Much Abides

A Survival Guide
for Aging Lives

Dr. Charles H. Edwards II

United Writers Press
Asheville, N.C.

ISBN: 978-1-952248-07-8 (print)
ISBN: 978-1-952248-10-8 (ebook)

Published by:
United Writers Press
Asheville, N.C.
www.unitedwriterspress.com

Cover painting:
Charles Edwards
Late, 2020
Oil on canvas

Images appearing at the beginning of each chapter
were also derived from paintings by the author.

Sales from this book support
Memory & Movement Charlotte.

Printed in the U.S.A.

This book is dedicated to my patients and their families. They have taught and continue to teach us what the human spirit looks like at its best.

Contents

Author's Note

Several idiosyncrasies in the book need to be addressed.

Throughout the book are passages in *italics*. These indicate when the reader is talking back to me, the author. We are covering sensitive and personal aspects of our lives together. This feature ensures that the reader and his perspective remain central in the discussion.

At the end of most chapters are endnotes relating to topics mentioned. These references are not meant to be exhaustive. They are offered as approachable sources for those readers that are interested in learning more about those topics.

I have led several workshops on aging where I present the material as *Common Mistakes In Aging*. Focusing on what not to do is an effective way to emphasize critical points and have them be remembered. I have addressed these issues throughout the book. By sharing them again in one place, I am repeating myself for emphasis.

I have done all the illustrations. It is readily apparent that I am not an accomplished artist and might have been better served by having a professional do them. But I insisted on this to make an important point. As we age, we must accept that we will no longer always be good at things. Time takes its toll on our talents. What is crucial is doing things that we enjoy and find valuable. If we limit ourselves solely to pursuits that we excel in, we will have lots of free time to mourn the loss of expertise. I hope you appreciate these illustrations as much as I enjoyed creating them.

The stories I share in the book are all derived from real people and experiences. Names have been avoided for obvious reasons. Time and memory are at odds with one another. Small details may be casualties but the major themes are genuine and factual.

I wish to express my gratitude to several individuals who have helped me complete this book.

First to my editor, Ken Garfield. He has provided the structure, guidance and encouragement to allow me to say what I wanted to say in the way I wanted to say it. He intuitively understood my passions and accepted my oddities graciously.

Second, I want to acknowledge my first editor, Julie Russell. She was crucial in convincing me that I had something to say that might be of value to others.

Third, sincere thanks to my friend Joe Cook for reviewing the manuscript and making suggestions.

Lastly, to the members of my family—my son Chuck, brother Mark, and sister-in-law Elaine. Thank you for caring enough about me to give your honest and valuable opinions. And finally to Mary, my wife, my biggest supporter and most thorough critic. Thank you for putting up with the process for two years and listening to all the versions. Your input was crucial to my finding my voice.

Much Abides

Tho' much is taken, much abides; and tho'
We are not now that strength which in old days
Moved earth and heaven; that which we are, we are;
One equal temper of heroic hearts,
Made weak by time and fate, but strong in will
To strive, to seek, to find, and not to yield.

— Alfred Lord Tennyson, from "Ulysses"

Prologue

ging is the ultimate human challenge. No one has ever made it as clear as Tennyson when he admits that our heroic hearts have been made weak by time and fate. Time takes its toll on every aspect of our lives—our bodies, minds, every thought, every dream. It is inescapable. Each of us will course through all the stages in life until the end. No one gets a pass.

The last stage—post-career, from retirement to death—is often undervalued and sadly wasted. This neglect is tragic because this last phase is as important as all the preceding phases. It is the time when we are finally free of the demands of careers and have time to pursue personal and often delayed agendas. If valued and approached creatively, this late phase has the potential to provide the most satisfaction and joy for the longest period of time. For all this upside, there is also the potential for not getting it right. For despair. The questions then arise: How do I avoid that despair and navigate this challenging late stage with balance and insight? How does one not mourn what is lost but make a life out of what is left?

That is what this book is about.

Three ideas, or themes, have merged to provide the inspiration to write this book.

The first theme is a lifelong fascination with stories. In my career as a physician, this would be the reminder that each patient is unique. This realization emerges as a technique to change patients' destructive behavior. We will start with a brief look at my story and how a late-career decision and pursuit changed me forever.

The second theme is the struggle I see in my aging contemporaries to finish their careers and find purpose in the word they cannot even say: Retirement. I have seen this transition done well, and I will share those stories. I have also seen this done poorly by friends whose lives, once rich in expectation and texture, are now uncertain. I am increasingly puzzled by the fact that we will spend years, often decades, preparing for a career that may last 30 years. But rarely are our post-career years, which often last as long, given thoughtful consideration. This omission is a threat to the successful retirement we all want.

The third and most important theme comes from my new career caring for patients and families suffering from memory loss. I have seen the aging process accelerated and become an illness, which paradoxically has sparked my interest (fervor is a better word) in normal aging. This is where the idea for the book took hold. Every day I see the effects of Alzheimer's disease on the memories, thoughts and behavior of my patients. It is a world of extremes. As the disease slowly peels off the social boundaries, confuses the context of relationships and erases the memories of life, the patient loses who he was and then who he is.

In this setting of decline, we often see the raw, unchecked emotions, anxiety and bizarre behaviors that make caring for these individuals difficult and sometimes impossible. Two insights follow: First, that aging brings on a similar decline for everyone to some degree. These lessons from the edge, from those suffering from dementia, can guide us in our own late journey. The second lesson from my patients is the key. Each of them had a story that ends tragically. Their voice has been silenced. If they could return from this horror, what would they tell us to value? What would they say matters? What gets in the way of achieving the peace and connectedness we all seek?

This book is intended to be a survival guide for aging lives. Just as in any long and arduous journey, we will all need guidance eventually. It is intended to be the welcome marker that finally appears when you think you have lost the trail. I will have failed if it is thought to provide specific answers to any one life. It is offered as a process that one can use to find answers for their own life.

No one has written on aging with more insight than Tennyson. In his poem, "Ulysses," the lines "Death closes all; but something ere the end, Some work of noble note, may yet be done" are as powerful and challenging to us as they were to Ulysses. The beauty of it is that we get to decide what that work of noble note is. To achieve something of note, the poet warns, we will need to "be strong in will." He ends with this reassurance, that "it is not too late to seek a newer world."

It is never tragic when something bad
happens. If you can use it in the right way,
it will buy you a ticket to a place you would
never have gone.

— Donald Davis[1]

1

The Storyteller's Story

I wrote this book because I had to. Long forgotten and suppressed aspects of my story have collided with a more recent disability, forcing me to become a different person and a different kind of doctor. These twists and turns led me to take a penetrating look at where I had been and what I wanted my future to look like. The uncertainty and, yes, the fear offered hard-earned insights into aging and life. Those insights became this book. Each of our stories holds a central place in how we navigate the challenges of growing old. I am asking you, the reader, to allow me to lead you on a journey examining your story alongside my story. We begin with parts of my story that are relevant to this journey.

I come from a long line of Celts. My father is Scots Irish and my mother is Irish. This exposed my brother and me to storytelling as an art form. Any family gathering or holiday was dominated by gripping stories told by my grandfather, father, uncles and aunts. They were nuanced, elaborately detailed and often hilarious yarns that addicted us early to their effectiveness in making life interesting and often magical. They explored human struggles, predicaments and ironies that focused on what works in life and what doesn't.

Underlying it all, these stories had the capacity to teach and inspire as well as caution. Simple neighbors could be elevated to hero status. Individuals of seeming authority and respect could be reduced to shame and ridicule.

I hear you already. **Who cares? Everyone, every family, tells stories. What's the big deal?**

The big deal for me was learning about others, where they came from, about their families and how they lived. For me, this curiosity was the beginning of that vital connection to others that makes life jump. I admit I have put people off with my quizzing. "You sure ask a lot of questions" has been said more than once. This fascination with personal narrative provided the foundation that would translate into my being a better listener as a physician and thus a more effective diagnostician. Finally, it led to the awareness that the power of narrative has implications for the changes in behavior that are required to age successfully.

My early years were dedicated to one undertaking, the passage of a round leather ball through a steel-rimmed hoop. Countless hours were spent practicing and playing basketball. Some proficiency resulted, enough to have hopes of playing Division I basketball for the University of Virginia. The hope never materialized. My college basketball career ended after one year. It had been everything and it was gone. I was devastated, and it provided me with the first real test of my character. When I called my father to tell him I had been inexplicably cut from the team, he said, "You just have to realize that you are not a basketball player anymore. Move on."

The quote from storyteller Donald Davis at the start of this chapter could not have been more appropriate for that time. The irony is that if I had made the team and become a star, as my dreams demanded, I would have never gone to medical school or become a physician. That failure, that humiliation, bought me a ticket to a place I thought I would never go, which was the exact place I was born to be.

Following graduation from UVa, I returned to North Carolina to enter medical school in Chapel Hill. I found medical school significantly easier than my college days. I hit my stride in the third year, when we began to interact with patients. The synergy of my hearing their stories, storing them in my brain and retrieving those crucial facts as needed gave me an advantage that has persisted.

I was born to practice medicine. It fits every aspect of my personality and intelligence. I frequently get the question, "What prompted you to go into medicine, then surgery?" There were no doctors in my family, my father being the first person in his family to graduate from college. I was the second. I had no idea what a career in medicine required or would entail.

The first hints that heart surgery would be in my future arose in my senior year at Myers Park High School with a boy named Gary Peine. Gary was a sophomore, lived down the street from me and happened to be manager of the basketball team. What was different about Gary was that he was a blue baby. He was tiny. His spine was crooked, which forced him to walk with an exaggerated limp. I would later understand that he was born with a congenital heart defect, Tetralogy of Fallot, that prevented blood from getting to his lungs. Hence the blue tint to his skin and lips. What really characterized

3

him was a love of basketball and being the manager of our team. I drove him home from practice every day and to all the games. Sometimes his mother would ask if I could take him to school. I have solid memories of his running to gather all the basketballs that we threw at him and then squatting to catch his breath. I would later learn that this was typical of patients with Tetralogy. I also remember him sitting next to me, talking nonstop about upcoming games and who would be guarding me and what happened the last time we played. After the season, we still rode some places together, but the frequency and intensity of the bond lessened.

One evening, I got a call from Gary's mother that he was ill and desperately wanted to see me. Would I have time to come to the hospital? When I walked into the room, I could see that he was weaker and bluer. He had oxygen tubes in his nose and could only speak in a whisper. He was too weak to sit up. I had to kneel down so I could hear. I told him he had to get well, that the team needed him. When I left the room, his mother followed me out. I asked, "Will he be OK?" She said, "The doctors give us little hope at this point." Then she added, "All he talks about is you and the team. Thank you so much for coming to see him."

The full weight of the situation hit me. I will always regret that I didn't fully understand how important I was to him. I was never anything but kind and protective, but I never engaged on that deep level that would have made him feel truly special in my eyes. I had missed some crucial aspects of his story. He was gone two days later. Kays Gary, the famed *Charlotte News* writer, came to school to write a story on Gary. He interviewed several of us who were on the team. One player told him that Gary was someone you looked up to. Kays Gary wrote in his final line, Gary Peine was 3 feet, 8 inches tall.[2]

Six years later, on a rotation in medical school, I was assigned a newborn who was born with Tetralogy of Fallot. She was going to undergo an operation to increase the blood supply to the lungs. I saw her in the crib, blue, and memories of Gary Peine painfully returned. The next day, the operation was done. I went to the recovery room. The baby was lying in an oxygen tent, but she was pink, not blue. The simple change in color to pink meant that now there was adequate blood flowing to the lungs. She would live. This was a miracle, and I wanted in on the miracles. From that moment on, I knew I wanted to be a cardiac surgeon.

I spent the next nine years at Duke University Medical Center training in cardiovascular surgery. This was an intense, demanding stage of my life. When finished, I was 34 years old and had performed over a thousand major operations. This crucible had given me expertise and confidence. I was ready.

My first job was an academic appointment in Los Angeles, California. I knew early that the life of an academic surgeon was not for me. An academic career requires an interest in research. I was given a large laboratory and responsibility for several research fellows. The path to success as a professor was in place but my heart was never in it. I did my best that year with the fellows and research, but on any given afternoon I wanted to see my daughter play soccer. I hate to be away from home. A life of travel and research was not for me. The trappings of academic success held no interest. Then divine intervention occurred. Presbyterian Hospital in my hometown of Charlotte, N.C., was given a certificate of need to start a heart program. They asked me to return to Charlotte to start this program. I was 35 years old. Things were moving fast. They never did slow down. For the next 29 years, I was given a gift. That gift was the trust invested in me by friends, former teachers, coaches, colleagues and fellow Charlotteans to care for and operate on them. It was a perfect match. They needed me to be prepared and skilled. I needed their affirmation to keep doing it.

The sphere around the sick is sacred. This simple statement has defined my career and my relationship with my patients. This reverence means having respect for the patient and situation, preparing for the operations, keeping up with new medical and surgical developments and being a respectful leader of the entire team caring for the patient and family.

I am a perfectionist and a worrier, a combination better suited to a psychiatric ward than a long career as a cardiac surgeon. All these factors—the stories, the worries, the perfectionist—melded to form a deeply personal and intense relationship with my patients.

I had a four-legged stool that rolled across the floor of the exam room. I'd roll up, put my hands on the patient's knees and say, "Tell me about yourself!" Often the response would be something along the lines of "I have this pain or symptom." I'd stop them. "We will get to the problem in a minute, first I want to know about you." What came next, the personal accounts and details of lives, made it not only interesting, but served as a constant reminder that this was not just another patient with chest pain. It was a person with a life who needed someone to fix their chest pain so they could go on with that life. It was the link that kept everything in perspective. I was a small part of their story. By sharing larger parts of that story, they became part of my story, the crucial part, that gave my career the depth that led to profound reward.

Sadly, many of the diseases I cared for that required invasive operations to address were the result of bad behavior. Smoking led to lung cancer and arterial disease. Reckless diets resulted in coronary disease and heart attacks. I became obsessed with how I could change patient behavior—to help them make better choices, to prevent the need for these huge operations or to simply prolong their beneficial effects. I would advise, cajole, threaten and even attempt to scare patients to see if I could change their destructive habits. Often my scolding would work for a while. But tragically only 50 percent of the patients would quit smoking and even less could sustain a healthy diet.

In midcareer, I had an epiphany while caring for a Penn State University football player who developed acute angina and had to have emergency surgery while on business in Charlotte. He had been a star linebacker for three years, playing in major bowls and for national championships. He was a household name for Penn State Nation. Even before the operation, he was reluctant to accept that he needed this emergency surgery. Post-op, the defiance accelerated. He could not come to grips that "Superman" was in this predicament. It was all in a blind spot. My post op pep talk fell flat, and I was not looking forward to the one-month follow-up. On that day, I entered the exam room and decided to give it one more try, with a twist. "Where is this going?" I asked him. "Where is your story going to end? A disciplined, accomplished athlete, a hero to many, plays out his life in restaurants and bars because he refuses to admit he may be on the wrong track. This is your story and only you can write it."

It did not go well. He left more defiant. Who was I to challenge him in this way? I didn't even go to Penn State! Two weeks later, a nurse came to my office door and said, "One of your patients wants to come back and talk with you." It was him.

"I have been thinking about you and about my story and I owe you an apology. You have been trying to help me and I have been a jerk. Ever since you talked about my story and that I was the one to write it, it has haunted me. I get it. I have suffered a health setback. But the best story is to accept it and move on. I want my story to be an example to others who have had the same adversity."

That is exactly what he did. He got into great shape and has mentored others with premature heart disease for 20 years. Once he understood that he had control over his story, the operation was no longer a tragedy for him or even something to be ashamed of. Rather, he saw it as that ticket to a place he would never have gone. Changing human behavior is still a challenge. But using personal narrative as a tool has helped me help many others.

Two years before retiring from surgery, I was operating one day and my assistant noted, "Dr. Edwards, your left hand is shaking."

My first response was "That can't be my hand, I don't shake." But it *was* my hand, and it *was* shaking. The shake persisted despite all my efforts to control it. It was never a disability and never had an impact on the outcome of an operation. But I was on notice that my plans to operate for as long as possible needed reevaluation. I was not going to be the old guy shaking in the operating room. Then came the despair. Misgivings about the future. Dark thoughts. Chuck Edwards is a heart surgeon. What happens when he is not a heart surgeon? All the preparation, sacrifice, skill—and, yes, affirmation—will be gone. One random day, I walk out a door and am not needed anymore. All this knowledge and wisdom, useless. Doom.

The fact that I would not be performing operations was not the main source of the despair. I loved being in the operating room and was always comfortable there. I prepared for the operations and cherished the entire ballet, especially the patient waking up after a successful operation. Complications were devastating. That perfectionist trait made me feel responsible for anything that happened to a patient I had operated on. Every patient was a teacher, and I continued to learn until the end. The loss of the surgical part of my career was not central to the forebodings about the future.

Central was the notion I would no longer see patients, be allowed to hear their stories or figure out what was wrong.

I decided to retire from surgery. I spent hours thinking of ways to stay active in medicine but nothing seemed remotely realistic. The future was out of focus, scary. Then a flicker of light appeared. My search for relevancy led me back to a tragic time in my family's history. My parents both died from Alzheimer's disease. Memories of being embarrassed, helpless to do something for them, surfaced. Even as connected as I was to medical care in Charlotte, we battled through every stage of the disease.

Our family struggles began when my father started to show the effects of memory loss at age 70. As is common with most families, looking back there were probably earlier signs, but they were subtle and easy to ignore. We had noted his asking repetitive questions and rapidly forgetting what had just been said. We then discovered he had not paid income taxes for two years. Several months later, he had the delusion that his long-deceased grandfather had come to visit with his dogs. We were going down rapidly. A valid question is "How could you not see the decline before it became starkly apparent?" As we see with our patients at Memory & Movement Charlotte, it is easy to mask the decline. Social skills remain intact until later in the disease. We knew he had become quieter, but my mother was still whole and she covered for him.

The worst of it was when he would suddenly get a look of terror on his face. At those times, it was apparent he did not know where he was or who we were. His story landed him on Omaha Beach in World War II, wounded him at St. Lo and allowed him to recover to become the example to my brother and me of what a man is supposed to be made of. Now the story was going to end with his not knowing where he was or who he was. I would say, "Dad, it's me, Chuck." I would hug him and slowly the look of fear would abate. Those moments when he was frightened and alone and I could not comfort him will haunt me forever. He was dead at 75 years of age.

My parents had sacrificed to send me to college and medical school. They were obviously proud of any success I had. It was deeper than that. They thought I could fix anything. My mother would overhear someone in a beauty parlor telling of a person with a medical problem related to the heart or chest and she would exclaim "My son can fix this." She would call to alert me that this family would be calling and they always did. I saw many of these patients in the office and sometimes I could fix it. Memory loss was different.

Their looks of despair and hurt would say, "Chuck, certainly you can do something. There must be somewhere we can go and get help."

I had nothing.

We all came together to preserve as much dignity as possible for my father. My mother was a different story. I was late in recognizing that dementia was slowing taking its toll on every aspect of her life. My parents were always generous with contributions. Every month she wrote a check to St. Jude Hospital in Memphis. We discovered too late that those monthly checks had become almost weekly checks. She was always one to stay connected with family and old friends and be aware of their needs. She slowly became reclusive and no longer initiated contact with friends. At this point, I was clueless and thought she was depressed about my dad. I would admonish her for not keeping up her correspondence and avoiding social events with her friends. She began to ask repetitive questions and exhibit rapid forgetting. We knew then it was Alzheimer's. She was unable to manage her life in the independent living of a retirement center and had to be moved to memory care. She became confused and finally psychotic, repeating the words "I want to go to bed" incessantly. I think what she was really saying was "I want to die." She was never put on antipsychotic medication, which might have helped. It wasn't that the physicians didn't want to help. It was a lack of time to listen, and a lack of experience in treating patients with dementia. My mother died in 1998. She was 76 years old.

When I allow my mind to travel back to those days of caring for my parents, the helplessness and frustration return. I realize that I had suppressed feelings of inadequacy. This search to remain relevant as a physician had led me back to my parents and those feelings.

The connection was made. I will open a center caring for patients and families struggling with memory loss. On fire with this revelation, I searched the house for my wife, Mary. She listened respectfully and responded as all wives of Irish Catholic men would: "Chuck, have you been drinking again?" After that world-record balloon pop, she added, "Look, you are the one who says all compassion begins with competence. May I point out that you have no expertise in this field. They already have family to hug them. What is needed is a physician who understands the disease and can treat its complications. You remember the pain we experienced with your parents when no one could help us? No, this is a bad idea!!"

Being married to the temple of truth is not easy.

It was not a bad idea. It just needed developing. I asked myself, "How could I get the expertise to care for these patients?" That night I started the application process by writing a letter, the first sentence reading, "When a 64-year-old cardiac surgeon applies for a dementia fellowship, it prompts the question, 'Shouldn't he be in the clinic instead of starting it?'" Maybe that line or subsequent explanation of why I wanted further training sparked a morbid curiosity. But something extraordinary was put in motion. The final result was my being accepted to several medical centers for further training in dementia. I chose Johns Hopkins University, where psychiatrists are in charge of the dementia service rather than neurology or geriatrics. I would need intense mentoring in psychiatric illness and psychotropic medications, both in the wheelhouse of psychiatry.

The process of certification was onerous. The fact that the ink had faded on many of my diplomas and certificates should have been a sign I may be late to the party. When I called the N.C. Medical Board to have my state exam scores sent to Johns Hopkins, the woman asked, "What year did you take the exam?"

When I told her I'd taken it in 1973, she sighed. "I can't produce those today. They will be downstairs in the archives. I will need some time to find them, if I even can."

She called back several days later, proud of her success in locating them. She said, almost incredulously, "You know, you did really well on this exam."

"Being old doesn't make me stupid," I said.

I arrived in Baltimore to start what was termed a "practicum." I met with my principal mentors, Paul Rosenberg and Kostas Lyketsos,[3] and was given the ground rules. This was an unusual situation for Johns Hopkins, never having accepted someone my age under these circumstances. They were intrigued with the possibility of retraining older physicians to care for the projected increase in patients with memory loss. It was explained that I would be accepted for up to six months and no credit would be offered. I would be supervised by staff and fellows and never have direct patient care responsibility. On the positive side, I would have access to all clinics, conferences and lectures. A specific curriculum would be developed to prepare me for starting a memory center in Charlotte. On my I.D., I was identified as a "psychiatric observer," whatever that is. From that moment on, I knew I would need humility and perseverance to survive.

There were times, especially early, that I doubted this was possible. I desperately wanted to come home. One week earlier, I had direct responsibility for the outcomes of complex cardiac procedures. Now that was gone. The first patient assigned to me at the psychiatric unit may have had the best read on the situation. She was a thin lady in her early 60s, lying in bed in the fetal position repeating the word "BULL&%IT" over and over. I thought at the time that this might be some sort of sign for me. I was humbled, but I persevered. The psychiatric fellows adopted me as a project. Days were spent in the clinic, attending lectures and conferences. Evenings were for reading and following up on what I was exposed to that day. The risk of failure became a source of energy. Slowly it began to sink in. The idea that this outrageous leap might be possible and result in the expertise to impact lives back home began to take shape.

One Johns Hopkins clinic that was especially valuable was Memory Clinic with Dr. Peter Rabins.[4] Dr. Rabins cowrote with Nancy Mace the dementia bible *The 36-Hour Day*, which has become the gold standard for caregivers. I asked him one day if he thought I could pull this off and become competent in memory care. He said, "Yes, but with one reservation. Heart surgeons are used to fixing things. You are not going to fix anything in this new career. Heart surgeons are used to having problems, big problems presented to them and they judge their effectiveness and worth by fixing those problems. Listening to patients is not a skill possessed by many surgeons. In geriatric psychiatry, listening is crucial to effectiveness."

Listening to all those patient's stories over the years gave me a head start. I carry that advice with me every day. After four months, Dr. Rosenberg said it was time for me to go home. "You have worked hard and come a long way. Now is the time to return to Charlotte, start your clinic and let the real teachers—the patients and families—take over your education." To the physicians and staff at Johns Hopkins who took time to prepare and encourage me, I am grateful beyond measure. The patients and families under our care in Charlotte, thank you as well.

After brief, failed flirtations with the two health care systems in our city, it became clear that if a memory center was going to be done right, it would have to be nonprofit and be independent. My wife, Mary, and I found 900 square feet of office space, upfitted it from flea markets and opened on Dec. 13, 2013. We had no patients, minimal funding and no idea what would happen.

What happened was that the phone started ringing. It has never stopped.

Note: The fate of the tremor and the Memory Center will be covered in the Epilogue.

Endnotes

1) Donald Davis, TEDx talk, Charlottesville 2014. This a short video of Donald Davis telling a story about his father. It beautifully demonstrates the theme of the story transforming the storyteller.
2) *The Charlotte Observer*, April 8, 1965.
3) Paul Rosenberg M.D., Professor of Psychiatry, Johns Hopkins University and Co-Director. Memory and Alzheimer's Treatment Center.
4) Kostas Lyketsos M.D., Professor of Psychiatry, Johns Hopkins University and Chairman of the Dept. of Psychiatry, Johns Hopkins Medical Institute, Bayview.

*This time, like all times, is a
very good one, if we but know
what to do with it.*

— **Ralph Waldo Emerson**

2

A Matter of Time

L et's start with a staggering statistic. Today in the United States, there are 95,543 individuals over the age of 100. In 2050, that number climbs to 800,000. (Yes, you read that right, 800,000.) That means there are going to be a lot of us aging Baby Boomers still alive in 30 years.

> ### Common Mistake of Aging #1
> **Underestimating the time left. For more than half of us, the post career will be almost as long as the career.**

We are all familiar with the statistic that the average life span in the United States has increased from 40 in 1900 to close to 80 in 2020. The year 2040 is predicted to be a tipping point, when there will be more individuals alive and over 60 than under 16. These numbers support what we already know. As a population in the United States, we are living longer. But what about you, as an individual? Today, if you make it to 50 years of age, then your recalculated life span is 80.9. If you make it to 65, the average length of life is 84. Seventy gets you to 85.

An 80-year-old can expect to live to 89 on average. The longer you live, the longer you will live.[1]

The real question is this: What determines longevity? Who makes it and why? A crucial study to answer that question was published in the *Archives of Internal Medicine in 2008*.[2] The study followed 2,357 men, average age 72, from 1981 to 2006. Of those men who were of normal weight, nondiabetic, did not smoke, had normal or controlled blood pressure and exercised two to four times a week, 54 percent lived to 90. For each risk factor, your chances dropped. If one had all five risk factors, the chances of living to 90 dropped to four percent.

There are two lessons to take away from this study. The first is that over half the participants who were in reasonable health lived 25 years after 65. The second is that most of the factors that translated into that longevity were the result of healthy choices, and in the control of the individual.

Who makes it? You do! You are probably going to live longer than you think. And if you make healthy choices along the way, you are going to live a LOT longer than you think.

But longevity by itself is not enough. What is it that we want from these added years? For me, I want them to be an endless sequence of days filled with joy, love and purpose. I want to be connected and relevant to those I love. When I am gone, I want to leave a big hole and be cherished for the bonds I had forged. Achieving these lofty goals requires more than healthy choices. It demands that we become aware of the factors that can enhance or undermine making that added time precious and valuable.

"If I could just do this all over again" begins countless, wistful sentences uttered by aging individuals. Sadly, it implies that the opportunity to actually do things over is lost. It is not! Twenty-five years is a lifetime. If valued and approached creatively, it can be a time of promise and potential. One can actually "do this over."

But "do over" comes with a price of admission. It requires an active process to unlock the essentials of successful aging. Understanding the science of aging and its effect on our brain is a good place to start.

Endnotes

1) Actuarial Life Table: Social Security Administration 2017.
2) Yates, Laurel et. al. Exceptional Longevity In Men: Modifiable factors associated with survival and function to age 90 years. *Arch Internal Medicine.* 2008 Feb. 11; 168(3) 284-290.

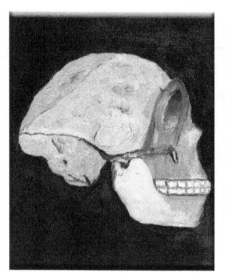 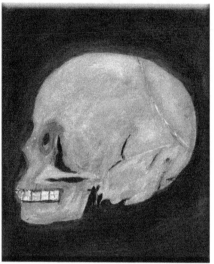

*Push back against the age as hard as
it pushes against you…*

— Flannery O'Connor

3

Why Does the
Science Matter?

I'm not sure whether Flannery O'Connor is talking about age in actual years or the period of time we live in, but it doesn't matter. What does matter is the realization that each of us is in a battle with time to remain relevant and purposeful. Just as in any battle, the more you know the enemy and its potential to harm, the better chance you have to push back against the negative effects.

We are going to start our counterattack by going back to school, science class to be precise. Every person is aware of how aging affects them physically. Fig 3.1 on the following page demonstrates the decline in time for certain races as the runner ages. This is no surprise to anyone. Professional athletes peak in their 20s and early 30s. It is rare for one to excel into their 40s. One look in the mirror is enough to convince anyone that time is taking a toll on our appearance. What surprises most individuals is the effect of aging on the brain and its function. Surely we get smarter and wiser with age. I know I am smarter and more insightful than my 43-year-old son!! Ah! Not so fast.

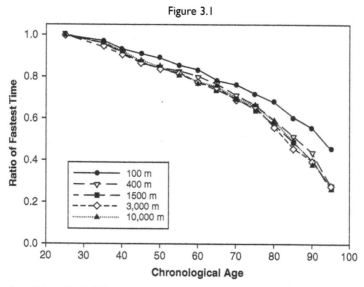

Figure 3.1

Source: Salthouse, Timothy A. *Major Issues In Cognitive Aging.*
Oxford University Press, p. 5

The irrefutable truth is that in almost every category of intelligence, mental performance declines in lockstep with physical decline. Fig 3.2 shows the performance of groups of individuals on various intelligence tests with advancing age. In all but two categories in this study, performance peaks in the late 20s and progressively declines with age.

I know what you're thinking. *I am going to live a long time but during that time I am going to get progressively more stupid!!*

Not exactly. To understand exactly how age affects our memory and cognition, we first need to learn more about the concept of intelligence. There are countless definitions, theories and studies on intelligence. For our needs and simplicity, we are going to use an approach first described in the early 1970s by psychologists John Horne and Raymond Cattell.[1] They divided intelligence into two categories, fluid

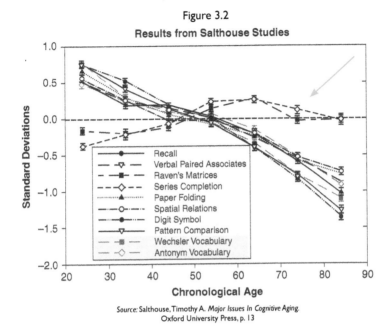

Figure 3.2
Results from Salthouse Studies

Source: Salthouse, Timothy A. *Major Issues In Cognitive Aging.*
Oxford University Press, p. 13

intelligence and crystallized intelligence. Stick with me here. It is simple.

Fluid intelligence is what we use to solve problems independent of acquired knowledge and life experiences. This is the classic IQ which peaks at age 28, then gradually declines throughout one's life. Yes, 28.

Crystallized intelligence gives us the ability to solve problems and apply cognitive skills based on acquired knowledge and life experience. It improves with age.[2] See Figure 3.3.

Wisdom would be an alternative description. Fig 3.4 shows a lifelong pattern of crystallized intelligence with multiple categories improving as we age. The graph shows improvement in scores with age in verbal comprehension,

23

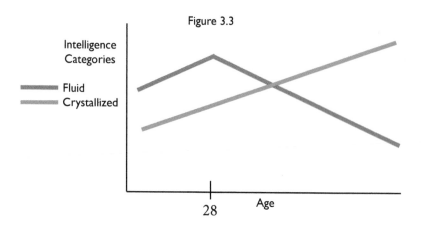

Figure 3.3

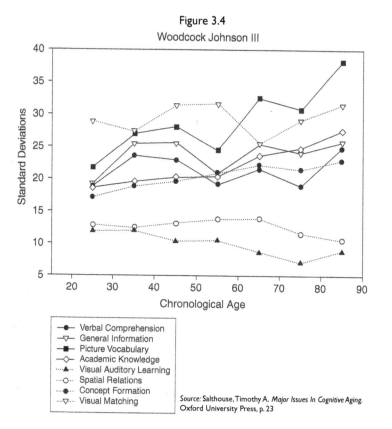

Figure 3.4
Woodcock Johnson III

Source: Salthouse, Timothy A. *Major Issues In Cognitive Aging.* Oxford University Press, p. 23

picture vocabulary, academic knowledge and general information, the cumulative effect of a lifetime of intellectual pursuits and achievement.

Why does any of this matter? If our mental faculties are impacted by aging, the more we know about the specific effects, the more we can use the faculties that are preserved to offset the ones that are in decline.

RGB is a 70-year-old friend who frantically calls one afternoon. "I am losing it and need to see you right away. My father had Alzheimer's late in life and I knew this would happen. I got it."

I ask, "What has prompted all this? I was with you three weeks ago and there was no sign that anything was wrong. I don't think this panic has been around too long."

He says, "Three things have occurred in the past two weeks that have convinced me that I am definitely losing it. The first two happened on successive nights last week. I often wake up in the night and have trouble going back to sleep. I will go down to the kitchen and eat a bowl of ice cream. On this particular night, I left the freezer door open. Sarah came down in the morning and was obviously upset that I had been so careless. The killer was, I did the exact same thing the next night. Now I'm beginning to doubt myself and she is rolling her eyes and thinking, 'Here we go.' The third clue was the hardest. I have played golf with the same foursome Wednesday afternoons for more than 10 years. We were teeing off and I realized that I could not recall the names of two guys in the foursome. These are my close friends and their names had left me! Gone! Get this, I had to sneak around their cart to look at the names on their golf bags. Are you kidding me!! I definitely have been slowing down since retiring. I am not as sharp with names. And forget about new technology. I lost the ability to turn on my TV with a new remote. I had to get my son to come over to turn the damn thing on. He put duct tape over one button that apparently can't be pushed or the TV can't be turned on."

We got RGB into the clinic and took a careful history, examined him and did neuropsychological testing. We sent off labs and did an MRI of his brain. Everything came back normal. We did follow-up on his difficulty sleeping. We were able to apply the best medicine—reassurance—and he went back to living his life.

This story is not unusual. Every two weeks, we get a frantic call from a patient insisting on being seen immediately because a memory lapse has them certain that dementia has set in. This panic is exaggerated if there is a history of dementia in a parent or grandparent. The majority of these "lapses" are the result of normal aging or the medical term "age-related cognitive decline."

Age-related cognitive decline is a term used to distinguish the effects on the brain from natural aging from the accelerated, pathological process of Alzheimer's disease and related dementia. Why does this distinction matter?

Let's look closely at the lapses experienced by RGB, our friend presented earlier in the chapter. He complains of not remembering names and having trouble with technology. These two processes seem different, but they share a common thread, which is key to understanding the aging process and our brains.

When you cannot remember someone's name, the brain goes through a search for the lost moniker. Everything about that person becomes apparent. Their face, all facts related to their life and how they intersected with you become immediately apparent—except the name. You have just experienced the battle between the decline of fluid intelligence and the preservation of crystallized intelligence.

The images that light up in the brain are the result of your history with that individual and are under the auspices of crystallized intelligence. The person's *name* is an abstraction. It has no connection to the actual personal involvement. It is an arbitrary label attached to the experience. Remembering names comes under fluid intelligence, which is declining from age 28. Natural aging will involve struggling for names.

The second lapse that sent RGB into a tailspin was technology. He lamented, "I lost the ability to turn on my TV with a new remote!!" Mastering technology is the sole domain of fluid intelligence. As a Baby Boomer, our life experiences were void of smartphones, iPads and computers. We never learned that pushing this button would result in this effect. My grandchildren, however, were weaned on those buttons and know intrinsically what to expect. The skill in our brain that is needed to manage even simple technology has been declining in us for 44 years. Predictably, technology will be a source of anger and frustration forever.

For all the reasons above, I state emphatically to patients being evaluated for memory loss, "I don't care about names or any technological lapse. It is part of natural aging."

If one is armed with the knowledge that age is affecting my brain in a predictable pattern, which results in changes in thinking and behavior, it allows that individual to be alert and able to compensate for certain declines. An awareness of what is age-related decline can protect an individual from the torment of thinking "I am losing it." The anxiety over memory loss can cause memory loss!

To understand fully the effects of time on the brain, we need to know what regions of the brain suffer the most from aging and exactly what that region does when young and healthy and what changes with advancing age.

The Prefrontal Cortex[3]

I am not exaggerating when I say that the emergence of the prefrontal cortex in the evolution of the human brain is the most important developmental advance in all of history. Period.

Please note the two skulls shown at the beginning of the chapter. The one on the left is from Neanderthal man. The one on the right is a modern skull (Homo sapien). Note the differences. The Neanderthal skull has a flat brow, but otherwise the two skulls are similar. The modern skull is projected out in front to accommodate the prefrontal cortex. Why is the increase in the size of this region of the brain so important for me to state that it is the most important advance in all of history?

Common Mistake of Aging #2
Being unaware of the effects of aging on the brain and how to adjust to them.

The role of the prefrontal cortex is the only proof needed to support this bold claim. The basic function of the prefrontal cortex is Attention. It has two basic components. The first is the ability to focus on a specific goal. The second is to filter out distractions that compete with that focus. This ability to concentrate and to process signals from the external world is the basis of all problem-solving. It also allows us to form memories, begin a sequence of action and engage in trial and error. The greater the capacity for attention and focus, the better chance of survival. The evolutionary advantage resulted in increasingly larger frontal lobes and the development of a deeper understanding of the external world, what we now call intelligence. It allowed prehistoric man to solve problems, to communicate with one another, leading to language, fire, the wheel, mathematics and on and on.

A commonly asked question is, "How do we know what a certain area of the brain does?"

There are several ways that specific attributes of the human brain can be localized to a certain region. The first is an awareness of deficits that follow injuries. Head injuries sustained in battle or in civilian trauma were the first evidence of the role of geography in the human brain. The second is the result of strokes. A stroke is caused by a lack of blood flow or hemorrhage to a specific area of the brain. Imaging can identify the region involved. Patients will exhibit predictable symptoms and changes in behavior related to damage in a particular domain. Thirdly, surgery performed to remove tumors or cure a seizure disorder involves the removal of brain tissue. After the operation, the deficits are correlated with the area removed. Through these insults to the brain, the function of a certain area is established by the deficits that result from the injury.

Executive Function

The term used for many of the characteristics of the prefrontal cortex is *executive function*. It is defined as the ability to organize a sequence of actions toward a specific goal. The prefrontal cortex is the center of intelligence in the human brain. It is where we are able to understand problems and act to solve them. It is where we assess risk and triage danger. An important feature in the prefrontal cortex is our ability to multitask. It is also the site of creativity, especially on the right side. It is where social boundaries are established and being aware of socially acceptable behavior. It is also where we control impulses. To sum it all up, teen-agers do not have prefrontal cortexes!

As modern humans, we are the product of millions of years in the development of the prefrontal cortex and the intelligence that follows. Unfortunately, the prefrontal cortex is the area of the brain that is most sensitive to the effects of aging. It can decrease in size by 10 to 15 percent in our 60s and 70s and is responsible for significant decline in our cognition.

Wait, are you serious? First you tell me that this one area of the brain is crucial to my being able to focus and solve problems and is the reason I'm not a Neanderthal. Then you shock me with the fact that these skills will erode with the shrinkage of this key area. Am I going to revert back to age 16?

Not exactly. What I am trying to do is make you aware of the effects of aging on your cognition and behavior so you can adjust. Those aspects of brain function that we attribute to crystallized intelligence can often show improvement over time. Vocabulary, reading comprehension and general knowledge are resistant to decline even into our 70s. The aspects of brain function that we attribute to fluid intelligence are sensitive to aging and show progressive decline from the 30s on. These include processing speed, ability to focus and to minimize distractions, the learning of new information (especially technology), problem-solving and psychomotor abilities.

Two critical functions that decline out of proportion are working memory and inhibition. Working memory is described as the scratchpad in our brains which uses short- and medium-term memory to complete urgent tasks and then is jettisoned. Visualize a young mother working at the stove, following a recipe for dinner while watching her young children play around her feet and at the same time talking to her mother on her cell phone. Each one of these tasks is being done effectively, evidenced by her reacting to a child moving too close to the stove. The ability to hold multiple thoughts and intentions in the mind at once is critical to problem-solving. Without it, one loses focus or gets out of sequence. This component of fluid intelligence, multitasking, is a major casualty in our struggle with aging. A young person can often keep multiple pursuits in focus at once, without slighting one. With age, holding two is difficult. Finally, one is a challenge.

A second major loss is the ability to focus and avoid distractions. The young mother, if distracted, returns immediately to where she left off in all the tasks at hand. As we age, we cannot stay focused in the presence of distractions. If distracted, we often have to start the task over. Inhibition is a crucial element of the brain which allows us to suppress socially unacceptable speech or behavior. It allows us to control our thought processes to enhance effectiveness. If the response inhibition in our brain declines, we are less likely to assess situations correctly and produce novel solutions to vexing problems. It forces us to repeat learned responses that may be dated or ineffective and can lead to poor decisions and, in the extreme, obsessions and compulsions. The goal obviously is to recognize the deficits that will arise from declines in fluid intelligence and use the wisdom preserved in crystallized intelligence to address and adjust for them.

Let me summarize by answering the original question, "Why does the science matter?" It matters because if we are NOT AWARE of the definite declines in our intellect brought on by advancing age then we begin to doubt ourselves. That doubt leads to a crisis in confidence and isolation. We see this too often at Memory & Movement Charlotte (remember RGB?). It matters because if we ARE AWARE then attentiveness and minor compensations can keep us keen and positive intellectually.

Strategies To Compensate For The Effects Of Aging

One of my early motivations for writing this book was to address a gap in the literature on aging. The scientific articles concentrate solely on the pathology, the specific effects on the regions of the brain, and the altered functions that result. There is no mention of how those alterations in function affect our behavior and actions. The pop culture articles make observations and suggestions as to how we should compensate for advancing age with no scientific evidence for their opinions. The challenge is to present the science in a form that is easily understood, and to use it as the source for practical strategies that allow us to compensate for the effects of time on our brains.

The science forecasts the following changes:

1. Tasks will take longer, some a lot longer. I often hear that "Balancing the checkbook used to take me an hour, now it takes two, if it happens at all."
2. Thought-processing will slow down. Solutions to simple problems will take more time. When participating in conversations, following the gist may be delayed. Tangential references or unfamiliar asides will throw us off. Getting it will take time.
3. Distractions will be more frequent and harder to overcome. When younger, we could pick up where we left off from the interruption. Now, we often have to start over. The frustration makes it more difficult to focus going forward.
4. Multitasking is a major casualty of aging. The days of executing three things at once are gone. It will soon get down to one.
5. Our ability to recognize errors wanes with age. The clue that something is amiss eludes us.

6. Remembering names will get more difficult.
7. Technology will require patience and mentoring. The improvement in our ability to function must be the goal. The technology has to have a specific purpose. We can grasp that.
8. Balancing the effects of aging with meeting the demands of complicated lives will cause anxiety. Anxiety and our goals of calm and purpose are at odds. Understanding the source of anxiety and ways to manage it are crucial to successful aging.
9. Will is the vital link between thought and action. It is the trigger for getting things accomplished. Will weakens with age and results in our not completing the things we desire. It is not important when it involves trivial pursuits. Haircuts, oil changes and golf dates can be missed without penalty. It is when we fail to connect with the essentials—children, grandchildren, close friends and meaningful events—that life loses animation and joy. Awareness of the decline is the first step in staying involved and remaining effective.
10. The relationship with risk resides in the frontal lobe. We have already covered the fact that the frontal lobe is the primary target of aging in the human brain. It follows that sound judgment in financial decisions is jeopardized by normal aging. Adding more weight to this assumption, the dementia which involves the frontal lobe is characterized by bizarre and irrational financial decisions.

Here's How To Compensate

1. Pay attention. Be aware of the effects of aging and introduce daily fail safes and strategies to offset the predictable consequences.
2. Slow down. Be less impulsive. Our brains are processing slower. Changes in our environment become harder

to note. Slowing down and double-checking provides valuable time to avoid errors. This is critical in driving, where errors are costly.

3. Work shorter intervals. Plan breaks. The ability to focus and avoid distractions depends on effectively managing time. Fatigue will lead to errors and frustration.

4. The ability to multitask and filter out distractions are casualties of the aging process. Avoid overloading schedules. Trying to take on too many things at once will make you less effective.

5. Make a commitment to complete what you set out to do. Set realistic goals, then complete them.

6. With important aspects of life, ask for help long before you need it, specifically finances. Involving others will do two things. First, it will avoid errors and sometimes a catastrophe. Second, it will bring loved ones and trusted individuals into your life. Allowing individuals to come closer opens avenues of trust and love. They must be developed early to have the greatest impact.

7. Don't be afraid to explore novel solutions to existing problems. The tendency with age is to apply the same solution over and over. It is still a problem because the old answers don't work. Yes, anxiety will accompany the search for new answers. But the positive effect on the brain is priceless.

The aging process is unique in each individual. These are guidelines to alert us to unwanted detours.

Every week at Memory & Movement Charlotte, we have individuals frantically calling, wanting to be tested for memory loss. Often there is a family history of dementia which heightens their concern that "I am losing it." The alarm is triggered by a lapse in memory that feeds into the underlying anxiety. We have them come in and go through our initial evaluation. The visit includes an interview with the patient and then the family, neuropsychiatric testing and a physical exam. We often will image the brain and always do a full set of labs. If appropriate, a carotid artery study is done. A significant percentage of patients seen will be considered normal with no memory or cognitive issues. They are diagnosed with anxiety rather than memory loss. We then have a counseling session describing how memory works and how it can be enhanced.

A metaphor in closing…

The process of memory can be illustrated by a file clerk and file cabinet. The file cabinet is the part of the brain where memories are stored. When information is needed, the brain knows exactly where it is to be found. It accesses the file cabinet, locates it and brings it into consciousness. Dementia destroys the file cabinet. It is no longer a functional part of the brain. No matter how hard a patient with Alzheimer's works to remember a detail, there is no place in the brain to store it. No storage, no retrieval.

Patients who fear their memories are defective but test normally have no problem with storage. They have a problem with attention. We use the image of a distracted file clerk to make this point.

The file clerk is you. It is your brain interfacing with the external world and deciding that something is worth remembering. The clerk marks it with a retrieval tag and stores it in the file cabinet. The file clerk has to be alert, be able to focus in depth and associate the memory with context.

Several factors associated with age can sabotage a file clerk and interrupt the memory process. Hearing loss is a major factor. Distraction due to sensory overload, preoccupation or self-absorption are often responsible for not mentally recording important observations or instructions. Anxiety for any reason can undermine the memory sequence. Anxiety associated with the fear of memory loss reinforces both the fear and the memory loss.

Retraining our personal file clerks to pay attention can dramatically improve memory and eliminate the anxiety that accompanies it. An added benefit is slowing down and focusing on the moment at hand. That makes us calmer and more effective.

Endnotes

1) Figs 3.1, 3.2, 3.3 are from *Major Issues in Cognitive Aging* by Timothy Salthouse. Salthouse has done elegant work on aging and his publications are available from Oxford University Press.
2) The Theory of Fluid and Crystallized Intelligence. Cattell, R.B. (1963) *Journal of Educational Psychology.* 54:1-22.
3) *Prefrontal Cortex* by Joaquin Fuster is a compendium of articles on the prefrontal cortex. It is approachable.

Is there anyone so wise as to learn by the experiences of others?

— Voltaire

4

Super Agers

L et me introduce SBA.

SBA is an 84-year-old widow living independently in a retirement community. She makes an appointment with Memory & Movement Charlotte, voicing concern over recent memory lapses. She arrives alone. She is medium height, thin, with short white hair. She smiles easily and admits to being overly anxious about memory. She explains that her father had memory challenges later in life, which has made her "a bit paranoid." She instructs us forcefully to "not go easy on me."

In the initial interview, she states that certain things have happened in the past month that have upped her concern about memory. "My whole life I have been good at names and worked at remembering them, but recently I have seen people in the dining room I have known for years and could not recall their names right off. They eventually come back to me, but it upsets me. Sometimes in the dining room, I will make myself recall the name of everyone I see just to test myself." She also admits to taking longer to make out checks and write letters. "I am always concerned about any errors and recheck everything several times." Her daily routine includes exercise, walking on the treadmill, swimming and golf. "I love to read, a book a week, and am addicted to bridge. I am taking a trip to Paris in the Spring and am taking French lessons. I have never been good at languages but it has been fun." She denies errors in managing money or missing appointments. She continues to drive without incident and bought a new, smaller car. She shares that recently her routine has changed because two close friends are in the Health Unit. She visits them daily. She takes medicine for high blood pressure but is otherwise in good health. When asked "What gives your life joy?" she responds, "Being with my children, grandchildren and my friends here. I am somewhat of a social chairman and I love to plan things. I hope I don't drive everybody crazy with my energy."

We give SBA two neuropsychiatric tests, the Montreal Cognitive Assessment and a Word Recall Test. She scores a perfect 30/30 on the MOCA and recalls 14 of 20 words—both extraordinary scores even for people in their 30s and 40s.

Obviously pleased when told her scores, SBA says, "How soon can I come back to be retested?" I respond, "You don't need us and probably never will." She is not a patient but we have remained close. She beams when I call her my Super Ager.

Questions arise. Does aging affect everyone the same? In athletics, there are those unusual superstars who dominate well into their 40s. Quarterback Tom Brady is a current example. Are there comparable individuals who defy the effects of time and continue to perform at the intellectual level of much younger individuals? The answer is a resounding YES. In scientific literature, they are referred to as Super Agers.

First, we need to define what constitutes a Super Ager. A Super Ager is the term first used by Northwestern University neurologist M. Marsel Mesulam[1] to describe individuals over 65 who cognitively test on a par with individuals in their 20s. A second feature of this group is the lack of atrophy (shrinkage) when their brains are imaged. In multiple studies, the percentage of Super Agers was in the 10-percent range of all participants. I suspect the actual percentage is much lower due to the bias created by Super Agers wanting to be tested. Not only was there less atrophy than expected for their age, but one area of the brain was consistently larger, the anterior cingulate cortex and its surroundings (ACC).

Why is this important? These areas of the Super Agers' brain that are naturally larger are the source of certain functions that control behavior and awareness. Two questions arise: Is the protection from cognitive decline due to the preserved functions? By being aware of these enhanced functions, is it possible to actively develop them and soften the effects of aging in our not-so-super brains?

The ACC is unique in its location and connections within the brain due to its involvement not only with cognition but more importantly, emotion. The function of the anterior cingulate cortex reflects that intersection. It is a primary source of attention. The attention takes two forms. The first is the awareness of the intentions of others. Being alert to individuals with possible sinister motives provides a survival advantage.

The second form of the attention is of oneself and your role in any given situation. The ACC is also intimately involved with the regulation of emotion and response to anxiety. Super Agers identify errors more readily and sense when "things just don't fit." They also respond to rewards, which is the basis of motivation and possibly competition. Finally and perhaps most important, they exhibit will, the juxtaposition of thought and action.

There is controversy in the literature regarding all the functions attributed to the ACC. But there is no doubt that it is a vital center, especially in attention and awareness. No one can question that remaining keen and aware into the later stages of life positively impacts the ability to successfully age. A patient who has sustained a stroke to both the right and left ACC would be pathologically passive and still. They would also be mute and indifferent to their surroundings, not even responding to pain. In his book, "The Astonishing Hypothesis," Francis Crick, who along with James Watson discovered the double helix structure of DNA, identified the ACC as the site of free will in the human brain.

A Super Ager walks into a room. He scans the room for context. Who is here? Do I know them? If I do, what do I know about them? This process is second nature and occurs effortlessly. The next thought is "What benefit can I derive from this situation?" The Super Ager absorbs the entire scene, noting what is unusual or striking. This is all done with detachment and calm.

You ask: *What does this have to do with me? I am happy that these Super Agers trump aging with a freakish preservation of this one area of their brain. But how does all this affect my brain and its daily chore of responding to Father Time?*

The answer to this question is crucial to our aging with grace and purpose. Super Agers are subconsciously more attentive and aware of themselves and others. Their ability to detect errors, control their emotions and act on thoughts and ideas is enhanced. We know that these characteristics ultimately result in some protection from the aging process. The question is whether we can CONSCIOUSLY become more attentive, more aware of ourselves and our interaction with others, and derive the same benefit. By controlling our emotional responses and closing the gap between thought and action, can we will our desires into being?

I know that the majority of readers at the start of this chapter asked themselves, "Am I a Super Ager?" That is not the question to ask. The question should be, "Is it possible by knowing the traits of Super Agers and the advantage that is awarded them genetically to duplicate the advantage in our brains by will?"

The answer is Yes! The benefit is a more energetic and engaged brain and a more energetic and engaged life.

Endnote

1) Marsel Mesulam, M.D. Director Mesulam Center for Cognitive Neurology. Super Aging Project: Northwestern University.

Everyone has a plan
until they get hit in the mouth.

— **Mike Tyson**[1]

5

Slings and Arrows

Boxer Mike Tyson is right. Life itself is that "hit in the mouth." It unfolds unpredictably, with every up, down and sudden twist taking its toll. We now are familiar with the physical and intellectual declines that accompany aging. But it is the emotional assaults that undermine our longing for peace and balance.

Medicine has a term for our orientation in space—proprioception. Simply defined, it is the ability to maintain balance and move safely. It depends on three factors. The first is our semicircular canals located close to the hearing mechanism. The second is our vision. The third is our spinal cord, which monitors our attachment to the earth and allows us to "feel" that connection. Ideally, all three work in concert to ensure that we are secure in balance and movement. If one of the organs malfunctions, the other two compensate. Losing two of these sensory functions results in vertigo, imbalance and often a fear of standing without assistance. This is an elegant physical system that compensates for attacks on our orientation in space. It fails only when two crucial elements falter.

You ask, *Are there three comparable centers that work together to ensure "emotional balance"—that sense our stress levels and adjust multiple factors to assure we are coping effectively?* Tragically, the designer forgot this feature. There are no passive internal adjustments to address the anxiety and uneasiness that come with being alive. The coping mechanisms needed to keep us calm and emotionally healthy must be active and constantly monitored. One must be aware of the forces that want to disrupt our desire for security and confidence.

Let's look at the factors that are evidence of internal turmoil. Being aware of them is the first step to controlling them.

Factors that Undermine Calmness and Purpose

Anger.

When I was performing heart surgery, I was struck by how common it was to see angry outbursts in my patients. It was frequent enough that I began to think it was a marker for heart disease. It may be. I became aware that individuals and families trying to navigate around anger were everywhere. It was devastating to all involved. In my practice with memory patients and those caring for them, I become deeply involved in family dynamics. I see the pattern persisting. The anger is always there. Only the triggers vary.

It took me a long time to recognize where the anger was coming from. The common thread is the resentment that somehow life has treated one unfairly. Each individual is unique in what they perceive is the source of the unfairness. But having gotten a raw deal at some point causes these uncontrollable eruptions. I am not saying that the perception of unfairness is wrong or even unjustified. The loss of parents at a young age or having parents incapable of responsibly raising children is tragic. But it shouldn't cripple individuals with anger.

Unfortunately, alcoholism, drug addiction and mental challenges often accompany the anger. Individuals affected by the enhanced outrage are often not aware of the source of the unfairness. But it is always a factor in their perception of the world. The process of working through the anger requires painful discovery. It often requires professional help to uncover the true source of the unfairness. Medication can be an option to help eliminate anger in any provocation. Quickness to anger makes dealing with the uncertainties of aging nearly impossible.

Anxiety.

If I could single out one factor that negatively influences us every day, it would be anxiety. Nothing else comes close. Understanding how difficult it is to get beyond this anxiety is crucial to achieving our goals for aging well.

The dictionary defines anxiety as painful uneasiness. I would add that it is the sense that something is not right. Something is amiss. I need to be vigilant. I should not let down my guard. The feeling is that of a giant hummingbird in my chest. The fluttering is disturbing. The sensation undermines our ability to focus and reason effectively. It demands our attention and robs us of relaxation and enjoying the moment. The body's response is "I want this anguish to stop!"

Anxiety enters our bodies in three ways. The first is early. We are born with it. It has been genetically selected for millions of years. If one is wary, anxious, we are less likely to go out in the night and get attacked by a mammoth. We are afraid to get close to a raging river and risk being swept away. One who avoids risky behavior has a better chance of survival and subsequently procreating. Caution is a marker for survival. Each of us is born with anxiety. It might not rise to the level of pathology, but it is there and demands to be understood and compensated for.

The second way that anxiety enters our persona is through traumatic life experiences. An accident, assault, rejection, loss of a loved one, all of these emotional experiences make us mindful that we don't want this to happen again. These setbacks intensify the underlying anxiety that we inherited. Most of the time, we are not aware of why we are anxious or even that we are anxious. But in certain situations, the anxiety becomes overwhelming. It becomes a disease. We are all familiar with Obsessive Compulsive Disease, PTSD, Panic Attacks and Generalized Anxiety Disorder. These are pathological and characterized by an excessive and constant feeling of being overwhelmed and in distress. Patients with these psychic maladies cannot function with this level of anguish. They require counseling, medication and, in the extreme, hospitalization. These individuals will do anything to decrease the agitation and often turn to medication, alcohol or illicit drugs "to make it stop."

Emotional hoarding.

The third entry is subtle, but cumulative and close to cruel. I call it emotional hoarding. Think back to joyful or even triumphant moments in your life. This is the night you starred in the school play, won the English award at graduation, scored 33 points in a basketball game or, the best one, when you fell in love. The warm feeling of reward and success flowed through your body and brain. You thought this fullness was divine. I want it to last forever. But these feelings unfairly and quickly dissipate. You still remember what happened, but the visceral glow is gone.

Now go back and think about the worst of times, the losses, the humiliations. These thoughts involve memories that are stored in your brain with searing emotions. They may be major events—the loss of a loved one, an injury or a romantic rejection. The visceral reaction, the churning stomach, the tingling skin or the hanging of the head occurs each time you go near that memory. This same reaction is associated with minor mishaps. It may be a time when you stupidly made a comment that embarrassed you or unintentionally hurt another's feelings.

It is tragically unfair: The positive, emotional rush from the high times, life finally coming close to enchantment, is gone. But cruelly, emotional baggage from the low points are forever stored emotionally in our brains. When recalled, we return to the hurtful throes of the sadness or embarrassment.

Over a lifetime, we are hoarding (excessively collecting to our detriment) emotions. This contributes to background anxiety that constantly distorts our perspectives and behavior, often without our realizing. Decisions or actions that seem illogical are the result of the hidden effect of anxiety on our thought processes. It is imperative that we become aware of the sources of our personal anxieties. It is Step One in resolving the conflicts. The process of resolution is the subject of a later chapter.

The problems we turn to and face are the problems of today; the problems we avoid and cower from are the problems of *every* day.
— Paraphrased from T. S. Eliot —

One major source of background anxiety is family conflict. We deal with it almost daily at Memory & Movement Charlotte. It is a source of uneasiness, agitation and often anger, all three undermining our quest for peace in the later stages of our lives.

Here is what it looks like in action:

I am introducing the concept of **Take Charge** to the daughter of a patient. This technique is when the caregiver identifies every one of their needs in caring for the patient, then actively recruits help from all available sources. It is designed to make caregivers more effective and less isolated. I ask her about her family.

"I have a brother and a sister," she answers. "Both live in nearby cities."

I ask if her sister can be more involved.

"My sister and I had a falling out and do not communicate easily."

"What was the falling out over?"

"It will seem silly to you now but it was over a desk. My grandmother had an antique Governor Winthrop desk. It was a centerpiece in her house. It was cherished by the entire family. Just before my grandmother died, my sister asked her for the desk. When she died, my sister got the desk. I was hurt and angry and said some things I probably shouldn't have. The end result has been that our relationship has never been the same."

"What happened to the desk?"

"I don't think she has it anymore. I really don't know where it is."

"Let me get this straight. You not only lost the desk, but you lost your sister. What is worse is that this has been a source of hurt and anger for years."

Tearfully, she nods. "Yes."

You might think that something as trivial as a spat over a desk deteriorating into a lifelong grudge between sisters is an exaggeration. It is not. The exaggeration is the pain and disruption that arise from family conflicts, however trivial. The expectation is that family is the source of love and acceptance. When that is not the reality, the gap causes anger and resentment. Some family conflicts cannot be resolved. The offense is too egregious, the damage too severe. But where it can be reconciled, the drop in anxiety and the resulting calmness is worth the initial uneasiness in reaching out.

We have defined anxiety and established how it enters our lives. The next step is to examine how it changes our behavior.

The primary effect is fear. What is it in our lives that we are afraid of? As a child, we are afraid of monsters, clowns, darkness. These fears affect our behavior. But eventually we realize that our fears are out of proportion to the possible danger and we grow out of them. Fear in adults is different. The stakes are raised. Forebodings are the result of life experiences gone awry. Memories of those misadventures are stored in our brains with raw emotion. Any thought or trigger that puts us near that emotion evokes anxiety. If the experience was traumatic enough, that anxiety accelerates to fear.

A young woman is involved in an auto accident on a rainy night. As an older woman, she refuses to drive in the rain or at night. A young man is cheated in a business deal. He subsequently avoids any investment with risk, forever. Examples abound. Fears which accumulate over a lifetime control our behavior. Some we are aware of, some not.

When I give talks on aging, I often begin with a question to participants. What is an overriding fear in your life? I would include such major experiences as a fall resulting in injury, developing cancer or being diagnosed with dementia. The consistent fear in multiple settings was always the same: "Running Out Of Money." This shocked me. Yes, running out of money is something to avoid. But to cause this level of anxiety, I needed to dig deeper.

Each of us has a unique and complicated relationship with money. It is an amalgam of life experiences that include parental influences, life's successes and failures, keeping up with the Joneses and on and on. It strikes at the core of our hopes, identity and security. It also has the potential to become an obsession, to postpone joy in pursuit of money. The answer to the question, "How much money does one need?" should NOT be "Just a little bit more."

Common Mistake of Aging #3
Having an unhealthy relationship with money.

When it comes to the management of money in the later stages of life, I am a disciple of Stephen Pollan, author of the book *Die Broke*. His simple financial advice is to enjoy your money, help your children in responsible ways and, lastly, "bounce the check to the undertaker." I offer this philosophy with some exaggeration, but not much. The harsh truth is that if the money you have saved cannot be turned into joy in your life or the lives of those you love, then it is a mirage. It doesn't exist. It is numbers on a piece of paper that arrives in the mail at the end of each month. Once basic concerns are met, the increasing number only satisfies an obsession. It has no true impact on our lives. In the search for grace and balance, a healthy relationship with money is crucial.

The manifestations of anxiety and fear are infinite. Each one of us has our own demons that we try to hide from the world. Often we are so good at the charade, we succeed in hiding them from ourselves. Two traits that develop in response to anxiety are common and particularly harmful. They are destructive both to the person exhibiting them and to those around them.

The first is **impatience.** Impatience is an intense desire for relief or change, restlessness. The impatient person says, "I don't like this moment (for whatever reason). I eagerly anticipate the next moment. The ensuing period of time will be better. I will be less anxious, calmer." If this pattern plays out, there is a continual loss of the present. Everything important in our lives can only happen in this moment. Love, kindness, understanding and the connection to others is at hand only in the present. Impatience has the potential to rob us of the potential that this moment promises with the illusion that the future holds more promise. Sadly, the next moment never comes. We are denizens of the present and must make the best of it.

The second destructive trait is **distraction.** Distraction is defined as dividing attention, a lack of intentional focus to what is present. Distraction is not the result of anxiety. It stems from a self-absorption that is common in aging individuals: Putting your needs and priorities first, to the detriment of others.

The picture that comes to mind is a family having dinner. The wife is serving and the children are excitedly sharing the happenings of the day. The father is sitting at the head of the table noticeably not paying attention to the theater in front of him. Something else is on his mind. He is not here. Not only is the father missing a chance to participate in the lives of his children but he is sending a dismissive signal to all who are part of the setting. The message to the family is "We are not valued. We cannot hold our father's attention. He has more important things in his life than us." If the father is attentive and participates in the family drama, the children realize they are valued. "What is going on in my life matters" is what they think. This translates into confidence and self-assurance. The opposite results in self-doubt and lack of confidence.

Each one of us on occasion will exhibit impatience and distraction. It is part of life's normal interactions. Heightened anxiety masquerading as impatience or selfish absorption, both associated with aging, can result in behavior detrimental to the exhibitor and those around them. The central character is often not aware. Being attentive to the present is fundamental to the struggle to stay relevant.

Medical Warnings

Medical diseases will dominate aging if not addressed. We learned in Chapter Two that controlling hypertension, smoking and body weight in conjunction with regular exercise results in dramatic longevity. Three medical entities, if not confronted aggressively, will rob individuals of time and quality of life. When I address these maladies in my patients with Mild Cognitive Impairment and early Alzheimer's disease, I see measurable improvement in cognition and memory almost immediately.

The first is **hearing loss.** A 2018 article in the British medical journal *The Lancet* identified hearing loss as the single most predictable marker for the onset of dementia.[3] It was considered more vital than genetics or vascular disease. Two factors result from the loss of hearing. The obvious one is social isolation. The second is not well understood. Apparently there are protective elements of sound waves being converted to electrical signals that keep crucial areas of the brain healthy and vibrant. The technology now available to compensate for decline in hearing is more individualized and effective. Anyone who suspects a decline in hearing should not ignore it. At our clinic, hearing loss goes hand in hand with dementia.

The second medical entity is **sleep apnea.** Healthy sleeping patterns are vital for all aspects of aging. Energy, mood and memory are integrally related to the amount and quality of sleep. In the past 20 years, a new science has emerged concerning sleep and the pathological states that surround it. Sleep apnea is the term used to describe abnormal patterns of sleep characterized by obstruction of air flow, buildup of carbon dioxide and cessation of breathing. The end result is an hypoxic insult (too little oxygen) to the brain every night that cumulatively causes permanent damage to the brain. Warning signs are loud snoring and apneic spells, when the individual stops breathing for alarming intervals. Any suspicion of sleep problems should trigger an evaluation by a sleep specialist. We have seen dramatic improvement in cognition following treatment for sleep apnea.

The third medical entity is **depression.** This is a complicated subject, and a deep discussion of the cause, effects and treatment are beyond the scope of this book. Healthy aging requires the navigation of some of life's most challenging events: Retirement and the perceived loss of value, loss of energy and skills, grief from the loss of loved ones or simply leaving a home that has been the center of life for generations. These are not maybes but certainties. Loss and the emotional effects can result in depression. Signs of the depression may be hidden and expressed only in tangential signs.

Common Mistake of Aging #4

Not recognizing the subtle signs of depression in the aging individual.

A young person with depression characteristically shows signs of sadness. It often is evident in his physical carriage and response to the external world. A lifetime of ups and downs in a "buck-up" world has made us masters at hiding our true thoughts and moods. The mask we don to hide our emotions and fears alter the signs of depression in aging individuals. Sadness may not be present. Often it is replaced by irritability, insomnia or fatigue. Relationships suffer and fracture. No one, neither the individual nor the family, is aware of the underlying cause of the changes in behavior.

Two symptoms warrant emphasis: **Apathy** and **anhedonia.**

The difference in the two is slight. Apathy is loss of interest in the details of life. Anhedonia is the loss of pleasure from pursuits that were formerly enjoyable. Apathy is often thought to accompany aging as interest in ideas, relationships, events and rituals decline naturally with the passage of time. This is a dangerous misconception. Keen interest in all aspects of life should not wane with time. If evident, it is a sign of pathological aging, including depression and possibly Alzheimer's or a related dementia.

The anhedonia is tragic. Losing what gave your life texture and joy is losing who you are. The response "I don't want to do things I once lived for because I am no longer good at them" indicates a refusal to accept the realities of aging. A disconnect from the stage of life we are in and refusing to adapt to new realities is the source of isolation, depression and despair. It also prevents individuals from getting help that would right the ship and return the potential for happiness.

Resistance to seeking treatment is seeded in misconceptions about what treatment looks like. The statement "I am not taking any medication that is going to change who I am" is a common refrain. The goal of treatment is not to change but to restore the patient to who he really is. Often no medication is needed. Psychotherapy designed to make the patient aware of failing defense mechanisms that result in isolation and anxiety is enough to improve the situation. If medication is indicated, it is targeted to the individual needs of the patient. A short course can reduce anxiety, elevate mood and soften irritability and anger.

Loneliness

If we are exploring the factors that undermine peace and purpose in our advancing years, loneliness stands out. It is important to note that being alone does not necessarily make one lonely. The opposite is also true. One can be lonely when not alone. Multiple studies have shown an increase in dementia in individuals answering "Yes" to the question, "Are you lonely?" This dementia is not Alzheimer's disease, and more research is needed to solidify the link between loneliness and dementia. Being aware of the health consequences of being lonely is a start. This must be coupled with communities and, specifically, health care professionals being aware. Counseling for these individuals and families can produce options for resolving the isolation. [4,5,6]

We started out with philosopher Mike Tyson warning us of what is to come. Life is going to "hit us in the mouth" more than once. Evidence of these blows—anger, depression and anxiety— have the potential to throw us off course, undermining our goal of aging with grace and purpose. Being aware is the first step in fighting back. The next step is to understand the factors that protect us from the downside of aging and give us a better shot at success.

Endnotes

1) Mike Tyson: Philosopher and World Heavyweight Champion (1987-1990).
2) Pollan, Stephen and Mark Levine. *Die Broke. A Radical, Four Part Financial Plan*. Harper Business Reprint, 1998.
3) www.thelancet.com Vol 391, April 21, 2018.
4) Loneliness In Older Persons. *Archives Int Med.* 2012, 172 (14): 1078-1084.
5) Loneliness and the risk of dementia. *J Geron B Psychol Sci Soc Sci.* 2018, Oct 26.
6) Loneliness and Risk of Alzheimer's Disease. *Archives of General Psychiatry.* 2007 Feb; 64 (2): 234-40.

By the time you get close to the answers,
it's nearly all over.

— Merle Haggard

6

Protection and Control

OK, I got it. I am going to live longer, maybe longer than I want. I now know that aging will do a job on my brain, which will cause me all kinds of problems. I really didn't need Mike Tyson to tell me life is hard, I am living that every day. But you made promises about success in the later stages of life. I like the sound of being loved and valued by my family and friends. But I am discouraged by the apparent lack of control that I have over what happens to me. If you can give me some direction, a few strategies, things I can control, then I will read on. But if, after exercising, being skinny and not smoking, this is nothing but a reckless game of chance, I'm out.

I hear you. I apologize for both the tedious science and depressing downside. But stick with me. I did make promises about successful aging and I plan to deliver. In my defense on the science, without it, all this is just hot air.

My career as a memory specialist has provided me with a stark realization. There is no aging with grace and purpose in my patients who are suffering from dementia. So protection from memory loss is central to any strategy of aging. We are going to cover scientifically proven pursuits that protect our brains from pathological decline. They also protect us from the certain declines that accompany normal aging.

Early Intervention for Blood Pressure and Lipids

The data is irrefutable. Controlling blood pressure and lipid abnormalities prevents arteriosclerosis and subsequent heart attacks and strokes. The earlier the intervention, the more pronounced the benefit. The crucial question for our purposes is, "Do these same strategies also protect our brains from developing dementia?" The science behind both these claims comes from the small town of Framingham, Massachusetts.

In 1948, the National Institutes of Health initiated a study to better understand the cause of heart attacks and strokes. They chose Framingham for the study. In the beginning, they enrolled 5,209 participants and exhaustively followed every aspect of their health. Patterns quickly emerged that identified patients who carried higher risk for cardiovascular events. Patients who smoked and had high blood pressures or high cholesterol suffered cardiovascular events at an accelerated rate. The term "risk factor" came from these early observations. What came next set the standard for care for patients throughout the world. The physicians began to aggressively treat hypertension and, for the first time, lower cholesterol. Smoking cessation programs were instituted. The result was an improvement in the overall health of this tiny burg. The rate of heart attacks, congestive heart failure and strokes began to drop. When results of the interventions in the Framingham Heart Study were published, those interventions became the model for the entire country.

Of interest to us is the effect that the aggressive control of risk factors had on the incidence of dementia. Beginning in 1975, the study was extended to follow the incidence of dementia. They now have reported over three decades, and the incidence of dementia fell in each successive decade. By comparison, the rate of Alzheimer's and related dementia in the general population doubled every five years after age 65.

There are many possible reasons for this decline in dementia. But a major reason is connected to controlling blood pressure and lowering lipids. The treatment of hypertension is a major objective at Memory & Movement Charlotte. A common obstacle for us is "white coat syndrome." This is when the patient thinks they only have elevated blood pressure in the doctor's office. In large studies, strokes and heart attacks are much more common in patients who mistakenly think the white coat is the problem. A recent study revealed how important even small elevations in blood pressure can be.[1, 2] The Sprint study focused on systolic blood pressure (the top number). The group with the target systolic blood pressure of 140 had significantly more strokes and heart attacks than the groups for which 120 systolic was the target. The takeaway here is that blood pressure should be a priority in any medical evaluation. The consequences of untreated or inadequately treated hypertension are too costly.

In 1986, a new class of lipid-lowering drugs were released. They are referred to as statins. They have two major functions. One is to dramatically lower lipids. The second has an anti-inflammatory effect. We continue to use statins in our patients with Mild Cognitive Impairment and early stages of dementia. The anti-inflammatory effect is most important in those early stages.

Exercise

The protective factor that is most supported by science is exercise. Let me start with a confession. When I was first introduced to the fact that individuals who regularly exercised had a lower incidence of Alzheimer's disease, I was skeptical. My smug reasoning was that these studies had an inherent bias that made their claims indefensible. The first sign of dementia is often depression accompanied by apathy. "There are no apathetic people in gyms." I was right about that but wrong on the exercise.

Common Mistake of Aging #5
Not valuing exercise. Thinking that the small amount I am capable of is of no benefit.

The science to support these claims came out of Carl Cotman's lab at the University of California, Irvine in the mid-1990s. They isolated a substance, BDNF (brain-derived neurotropic factor), which was released from the brain and skeletal muscle during exercise. A series of experiments followed where BDNF came in direct contact with neurons (brain cells). The neurons dramatically increased in size and in their interconnections with other neurons. This offset the usual pattern of aging neurons shrinking in size and exhibiting fewer interconnections. There it was—the first reproducible scientific link of exercise with a cellular effect on the neuron. That breakthrough ignited an entire new field of research. Thousands of articles extolling the benefits of exercise in preventing dementia followed. The research also proposed a positive effect of exercise on depression and psychosis.

John Ratey, a Boston psychiatrist and clinical professor at Harvard University, wrote the book, *Spark: The Revolutionary New Science of Exercise and the Brain.*[3] In it, he reviews this history and presents the science in a balanced manner. He has called BDNF "Miracle-Gro" for your brain. Ratey also makes the point that any exercise up to a point is beneficial. He pushes strenuous sessions several times per week as being optimal.

Those of us who don't get the sacred endorphin high will be pleased to know that there is a limit to the positive effect. Those individuals obsessed with pushing beyond reasonable limits may not get any additional benefit over us saner individuals. The exercise crazies do a great disservice by discouraging the rest of us from rational levels of effort.

Here's how that works. You decide to get into shape and run/walk a 5K. You finish and get to your car with the afterglow and a 5K sticker to put on your car. You notice the guy in the next space has a 10K sticker. The glow diminishes slightly with the comparison. Being competitive, you commit to a 10K yourself. But all over, you notice 12.5K stickers, then 26-mile stickers and finally a 100K sticker. You say, "What the hell!" So you take up biking. You start with a 10-mile ride in normal shorts on a classic wide-tire bicycle. It is impossible not to notice other bikers chuckling over your naivete. They are dressed in strange shorts with protuberances out the back, and they think you look funny. They clip themselves into the pedals to give them "leverage," not realizing they have converted a bicycle into a death trap. Instead of riding for exercise and enjoyment, they have to ride from New York to Chicago in four days. You again feel diminished and begin searching for other diversions. We must remember that the person with the worst Obsessive Compulsive Disorder will dominate the agenda until challenged. In exercise, we need to start slow and have reasonable expectations.

The science to date supports lifelong patterns of moderate exercise as protection from Alzheimer's and related dementias. It also has the added benefit of energy, calmness and a sense of well-being. Few things in life offer more promise.

Social Interaction

Now to the good stuff. You wanted control over what happens to you, a certainty that if I do this, I have a good chance of getting the result I expect. Is this possible?

Yes, and there is science behind it. Specific choices one makes over a lifetime evolve into characteristics that result in happier, healthier lives.

Two landmark studies support this claim.

The first is the Harvard Study of Adult Development, which followed two groups of men for 80 years beginning in 1938.[4] The first group included 268 Harvard sophomores (future president John Kennedy was one). The second group was made up of 456 inner-city boys from Boston ages 12 to 16. Every two years, the study reevaluated each of the participants in-depth—drawing blood, reviewing medical histories and interviewing the participants and their significant others. What emerges is a fascinating look into entire lives. This allows not only the ability to track health outcomes, but more importantly, what the participants thought about their success, happiness and overall well-being. The current director of the ongoing study, psychiatrist Robert Waldinger, has written and lectured on several aspects of the data. He draws three major insights:

1. The men with close relationships with family and friends reported being happier and were noted as being healthier. The reverse was also dramatic. Participants who stated being lonely were less healthy and less happy. Waldinger says emphatically, "The loneliness was toxic."

2. In the early years of the study, participants felt the number of friends was important. By middle age the quality of the relationships dominated. Couples that reported marriages marked by conflict and low affection were less happy than divorced couples in the study. Individuals with supportive spouses and family were able to tolerate pain more effectively when injured and recovered more effectively from setbacks.

3. The men who were in stable marriages were not only happier but healthier. They lived longer. Most importantly, these individuals suffered less memory loss and lower incidence of dementia.

Waldinger summarizes: "It was not the cholesterol levels or the smoking history that mattered. The ability to sustain loving and supportive family connections was the source of these life benefits. The willingness to make sacrifices that are required to nurture these bonds over a lifetime resulted in protection from dementia."

The second study is known as the Nun Study. This is a remarkable look at the lives of 678 sister members of the School Sisters of Notre Dame beginning in 1986 and culminating in the publishing of the book *Aging with Grace* in 2002.[5] The principal investigator was Dr. David Snowdon, an epidemiologist at the Sanders-Brown Center on Aging at the University of Kentucky. The nuns, each 75 or over, were a perfect group to study Alzheimer's and related dementias for two reasons. The first was control of variables. There was no income or social status differences in the participants. There were no smokers. Everyone ate the same diet, shared the same housing and had the same access to health care. The second reason was that the majority of the nuns courageously permitted an autopsy on their brains at death. These two factors resulted in the first large-scale study which correlated life history, memory, cognition and independence as well as brain pathology at death.

The findings shocked everyone. The pathology at autopsy often did not match the details of the life before death. Several nuns were in their 90s, had intact memories and were caring for themselves. The shock came when these nuns had the same number of plaques and tangles (markers for Alzheimer's) at autopsy as the sisters who had advanced dementia. One would have expected that the sisters who were mentally intact and independent to show no evidence of the destructive process typical of Alzheimer's disease. At the least, markedly less.

In looking closer, the nuns who were spared memory loss despite having the pathology of Alzheimer's had certain traits while alive. They were consistently noted to have larger social networks. This included loving and supportive relationships with their fellow nuns, and also with their families and the world outside the convent.

There are multiple scientific lessons to glean from this elegant study. I want to focus on two that the author cited as impressive, but not measurable. Dr. Snowdon states, "The first is a deep spirituality that the women shared." My sense is that profound faith, like a positive attitude, buffers the sorrows and tragedies that all of us experience. The second factor is the power of community. The young women entering the convent gave up the possibility of a conventional life, marriage, children and close proximity to extended families. What they received in turn was a social environment that provided unconditional love. Coupled with that love was a solemn vow that they would be cared for with respect and dignity to the end of their lives. Each of the sisters was revered for who she was and what she contributed to the whole. There was also the assurance that she would not only enter heaven but also the hearts of those sisters surviving her, just as her predecessors had for more than 100 years.

Not surprisingly, there was a measurable outcome. This culture of unconditional love resulted in longevity. The School Sisters of Notre Dame lived on average 25 percent longer than the general public. This belonging, the vital connection to others, is at the core of the peace we covet. In these two studies, the numbers verify the happier, healthier lives that result.

I can hear you say, *I want that peace and calm in my life, not just for the longevity but I think it would make every day easier. I don't have to point out, though, that it is late for me to enter a Catholic religious order to get it. Can I get it another way?*

Read on to find out.

Education

A consistent finding in multiple studies on aging is the protection that education provides the brain. Those individuals with advanced degrees have a lower incidence of dementia than those with BA degrees. The holders of those BA degrees have a lower incidence than high school graduates who, in turn, suffer less from dementia than those who did not finish high school. In both the Harvard and Nun studies, the more education, the longer the life with memory intact. The inference that education is limited to attaining degrees and that those with degrees are smarter needs to be dispelled. I was relieved of this misconception early in life. My father, looking at my diplomas displayed on the wall of my first office, stated emphatically, "Chuck, I think you may be educated beyond your intelligence."

Dad, I hope you were kidding but you do bring up the key point in this discussion. The reasons an individual can benefit from education includes social status, family income, absence of health or mental disabilities and, finally, intelligence. The factors involved in those who are denied access or choose not to pursue education are also multiple. They include family concerns, racial bias, nutrition and poor decisions early in life. All this preamble on intelligence and opportunity sets up the question, "Why does education and specifically advanced degrees protect the brain from cognitive decline and result in longevity?"

The answer is not clear and the science is murky. The most common explanation is that education results in cognitive reserve. This is the ability of the brain to develop multiple, and sometimes novel, ways of solving problems. The theory is that education leads to multiple pathways to solve problems. The more education, the more pathways. The number of pathways becomes critical when we age and begin to lose neural connections and pathways. Education provides a number of ways to solve problems, resulting in protection from dementia. Whatever the reason for the positive effects of education, it is a fact. The question arises: Can we protect our brains by continuing our education? What form would this take?[6]

The measurable benefit involves classic education. It does not address the individual pursuit of education, which certainly would provide a benefit. It specifically involves the attainment of degrees, high school, college and beyond, though there are many other venues for lifelong learning and intellectual stimulation.

The classic approach involves the mastering of a body of material, often in a mentoring or lecture format. The individual is tested and if found sufficiently quick with the material, passes the course. If enough courses are mastered, a degree is bestowed. This is a slow, cumbersome process but one we know works for careers, and protects us from dementia. What we don't know are the determining elements in the process necessary to receive the protective effect.

You say, *Come on, Chuck. You wanted me to join a religious order and now you want me to go back to college. These are not rational strategies. It is closer to insane.*

No, I don't want you to pack up and head back to State College to reap this benefit. What I want is to emphasize how important it is to stay curious and to pursue learning. One can re-create the classic, proven approach by taking courses in your hometown. Community colleges and local universities offer adult education classes. Online courses are all over the Internet in subjects that will be of interest to those still interested in learning. To me, the desire to continue learning is more important than the venue. Voracious reading on a subject may suffice. Sustained curiosity is the key.

In our workshops, I will ask, "What was your favorite subject in school?" The answer often is math. I will follow with the question, "When was your last class in math?" The answer is either high school or freshman year of college even among those with advanced degrees in science. I ask, "Why?" The answer? "I had to take the prerequisites for my major and my aptitude for math got pushed aside and forgotten." The point here is that at this stage of life, you get to take what interests you. The time for prerequisites is over. You have already passed the course entitled "Life."

Math may be a stretch. But why can't a love of English or history be reignited? Will it be scary? Will I be anxious? Absolutely. But if you are studying new material and being tested on it, the brain is engaged, looking for new pathways to answer new questions. It may be French, art history, art itself or photography. The beauty of the whole experience is your deciding what you want to study and then doing it.

What if I fail the course? I will be humiliated.

It is the process that is beneficial, not the endpoint. Even searching your brain and coming up with the wrong answers can trigger the benefit. An added benefit is the social interaction and connections to people in the class with similar interests. New knowledge and social interaction offer a double positive for protecting your brain. On the first day, you will know you are on the right track when you see a nun sitting behind you.

The greatest discovery of my generation is that a human being can alter his life by altering his attitudes.

William James

Positive Thoughts

Attitude affects everything. It always has. The experiences one endures, good and bad, shape our outlook on life. They first affect our thoughts, then our actions. Unfairly, the bad experiences have more traction. Each bad occurrence is stored in our memory and results in cumulative anxiety and often anger. If one is attentive to our brain's tendency to hoard negativity then the process can be checked.

> ### Common Mistake of Aging #6
> **Allowing negative thoughts and anger to take a foothold on our life perspective.**

Let me give you an example of how this looks.

A young mother is driving her three children to school. The youngest has special needs and has been difficult on this morning. The family is late and tense. The mother is speeding and gets behind a car moving slowly and erratically. She immediately knows that this is "a little old lady" when a sliver of silver hair is all she can see above the seat. The car is now blocking a long line of traffic. It has slowed and moved toward the curb. The young mother has two options in dealing with this situation. The first is to spark with anger, to think of herself as a victim. This old lady has no idea how hard it is to get these children ready for school. She has no business being out this early when those of us with a purpose should have priority. These thoughts result in predictable action. She frantically checks the left lane and, when clear, she honks the horn and speeds by. There may be a hand gesture involved in the escape. The young mother's brain is flooded with the chemicals linked to impatience, anger and impulsivity. These chemicals have the potential to affect her behavior long after she forgets the "little old lady." The children watched this scenario and learned that when late and stressed, it is acceptable to be rude and unkind.

A second alternative involves completely different thoughts and actions. When seeing the elderly lady driving erratically, her emotions focus on the woman. What is going with her? Is she ill? This is dangerous! "You children stay in the car. I am going to check on this poor lady and see why she is struggling." Approaching the driver's side, the young mother notices that the right side of her mouth is drooping and she cannot talk coherently. She can only point and grunt. She is having a major stroke. The car is now off the road. After calling 911, she gets the children out of her car and the family comforts this woman while waiting for the ambulance. As the ambulance screams off, the young mother's brain is flooded with chemicals associated with calm, kind and competent. The children have a lifelong memory of what to do in similar situations. They also have an amazing "show and tell" story for their class that morning. You get the idea. Positive thoughts, caring thoughts translate into actions that reduce stress and increase self-worth. Both of these are factors in longevity and happiness.

Another question pops up: *Is there any science to back up your claim regarding attitude and aging?*

Yes, there are countless articles and books written on the subject. There is even a branch of philosophy called Positivism. One of the better designed studies linking attitude to health outcomes came out of Duke University Medical Center and was published in the Archives of Internal Medicine in 2011. Duke researchers followed 2,818 patients with heart disease for 15 years after coronary angiography. This is a dye test to establish blockages in the arteries to the heart during heart attacks. The attitude of the patient was determined by a questionnaire designed to unmask their view of the future living with heart disease. Statements were offered to the patient, who then indicated which statement better described their feelings about their new life: "My heart condition will have little effect on my life" or a negative statement such as "I expect my lifestyle to suffer because of my heart condition." After matching for multiple variables— severity of disease, sex, depression, smoking and weight— attitude was evaluated. A positive response to the questions resulted in a dramatic impact on survival. The patients with positive attitude had a mortality rate more than 18 percent lower than the negative responders.

Investigators proposed two explanations for the differences in the two groups. The first theory was that the positive patients were motivated and better able to follow their treatment plans. The second was that the negative expectations led to uncertainty, tension and stress, these being risk factors for the development of coronary artery disease. It is interesting that researchers linked positive thoughts with the positive action of following guidelines, which resulted in healthier outcomes.

A positive attitude is the source of positive thoughts and subsequent positive actions. This sequence produces chemicals in the brain that make us calmer and more effective in dealing with the challenges that life presents us day after day. Over a lifetime, this calming effect results in longevity and protection of the aging brain from dementia. Anger and high stress levels are linked to hypertension and the development of arteriosclerosis. This is a crucial link in the development of vascular dementia.

Evidence that chemicals in the brain actually respond to external events is offered in the study of tears. Much of our understanding of tears comes from the laboratory of Dr. William Frey II at the University of Minnesota in the mid-1980s and culminated in a book, *Crying: The Mystery of Tears.*[7] This work identified three types of human tears. The first are basal tears, which continually protect the eye and keep it moist. The second type are reflex tears, which react to a grain of sand or slicing an onion. Where it gets interesting is in the third type—emotional tears. These tears are the immediate reaction of the brain to emotion, suffering or pain. Tears shed from pain or sadness are chemically different from basal or reflex tears. They have a higher content of manganese, prolactin and a substance called leucine-enkephalin. This latter chemical is thought to be an endorphin, a calming substance released by the brain in different settings. It may explain the calm that follows the shedding of tears.

This matter of fact about tears is critical to understanding the interface of the human brain with the outside world. External events immediately change the chemistry in our brains. The change in the composition of the tears prove it. If our responses are consistently negative, the result is anger and isolation. Positive views of the world create chemicals linked to calmness and connections to others.

The six chapters we have covered so far have focused on awareness—the factors one must be aware of to successfully navigate the later stages of life. I have tried to provide enough science to give the insights weight. The focus now will shift to action. How does one actually navigate these later stages? One starts with the recognition that I am now in a different phase of my life. Change will be required to be happy and balanced in this new reality. That's where we head next.

Endnotes

1) Sprint Trial Results. *Hypertension.* 2016 Feb; 67(2): 263-5.

2) Sprint Memory and Cognition In Decreased Hypertension. *Blood Pressure.* 2018 Oct; 27(5): 247-248

3) John Ratey's book Spark is a good place to start. It is referenced for both the positive effects of exercise and BDNF.

4) Harvard Study of Human Development. The best place to start is the 2015 TED Talk by Robert Waldinger, the current director of the study.

5) Snowdon, David. *Aging With Grace: What the Nun Study Teaches Us about Leading Longer, Healthier, and More Meaningful Lives.* Bantam, 2002.

6) *Brain.* 2010 Aug: 133 (Pt8): 2210-16.

7) Frey II, Dr. William. *Mystery of Tears.* Winston Press, 1985

Time is a river, the restless flow of all created things. One thing no sooner comes in sight then it is hurried past and another is borne along, only to be swept in its turn.

— Marcus Aurelius

7

Transitions

Each successive stage of life requires new perspective and skills to flourish. If one entered the business world with the judgment and acumen of a college sophomore, careers would be in jeopardy. Success in each phase is determined by the realization that things have changed and I must change to stay relevant. This is critically true for the later stages, which demand definite changes in thought and action to maintain balance. One must continually be on the lookout for signs that transitions are imminent.

Common Mistake of Aging #7

**Not preparing for the eventual transitions in our future.
Refusing to adjust to the realities of aging.**

Transitions are when life passes into new, uncharted waters. Often these passages are permanent. No going back. The permanence stems from the cumulative effects of aging, erosion of skills, family stresses and retirement—the fundamentals of aging. How well these challenges are managed determines the potential one has to age successfully. Individuals oblivious to the changes and their permanence lose focus and clarity. To illustrate, let me introduce my friend RAM. The following conversation broadly reflects what was said.

RAM is a 70-year-old internist. He and I have been friends for more than 30 years. He is not only respected but revered for both his expertise and ability to connect with his patients. He never slowed down at 65 and only recently began to take one day a week off. He calls one morning and asks if he can see me late that afternoon. I took care of his father, who suffered from Alzheimer's. The short notice makes me apprehensive.

He arrives promptly at 5 p.m. He is nervous.

CHE: *What's on your mind? You seem upset.*

RAM: *Chuck, I am embarrassed even being here. You would think that after all the advice I have given patients over the years that I would be able to figure my own problems out.*

CHE: *You're the last person I need to be telling, He who treats himself has a fool for a patient and a fool for a doctor. Sorry, go on.*

RAM: *I think I have always been so absorbed with medicine and my patients that I gave little thought to when it would end. I guess I never thought it would. At 65, I still saw more patients than any of my partners. At 70, I was still carrying a full load. It was when I started to take the day off that the anxiety about the future kicked in.*

CHE: *You are the first guy in history to regret taking a day off. I never had you pegged as a workaholic.*

RAM: *You know me better than that. I always looked forward to my time off. I love playing golf with you guys and traveling with family. But the day off was different. I would wake up in the morning and think, "I can do anything I want today. I can play golf, go fishing, do yardwork, anything." Then my mind would fast forward to the future. Soon, this will be every day. What do I want that to look like? When I project into the future, the picture is fuzzy and sometimes blank. I have known every day of my life what I need to do or want to do. It was clear. It was as if the calendar for the remaining days of my life was already filled in. To be honest, I am terrified of what the future holds for me.*

CHE: *Have you talked to Ann about this?*

RAM: *Just in passing. On the day I am home, I am afraid to ask about her plans. I know she would rearrange her day but I don't want her feeling sorry for me. Being married to a physician is not easy. The calls, family disruptions and waiting are constant. She has built a full and busy life parallel to mine. It would be insensitive now for me to say, "I need your attention and want you again to subjugate your life for my needs."*

CHE: *I doubt she would see it that way.*

RAM: *She wouldn't, but I don't want her thinking Rod is running out of steam and needs my help. Either way, I'm screwed. I go do stuff I don't want to do just to get out of the house or I'm home for lunch with both of us eating pity.*

CHE: *I think you are way off here. Has it occurred to you that she might actually want to spend more time with you? After all, she did marry you so you could be together. The parallel life she has created is not because she doesn't want to be with you. It was a compensation for your being consumed. My wife Mary would be rolling her eyes right now if she knew I was giving marital advice.*

RAM: *Here's the part that's the hardest to swallow. I have spent my entire life studying so I would know the right answer. The right answer got me into Princeton, then Duke Medical School. Those answers ended up saving lives. So one day in the near future, I will walk out of my office and leave those answers, which are now wisdom, behind. I hear a voice saying, "Sorry, Rod, this aging is a tough business. You won't need those answers anymore because no one is going to depend on you knowing anything."*

CHE: *Everyone has to confront that day when their career ends. You are no different. Has something happened that has triggered all this emotion to surface?*

RAM: *It's lots of things. I know I am slowing down. It is taking me longer to get my work done. I am actually working more hours to get the same work accomplished. I am terrified I will miss something on a patient. There is pressure for us to see 30 to 35 patients in a day. I spend 12 minutes physically in front of a patient, which is not enough time to figure out what is wrong. It takes me longer to enter the visit in the electronic medical record than I spend with the patient.*

CHE: *Do you still look forward to going to work? Are the face-to-face encounters with the patient still interesting?*

RAM: *I hate to say this, but much of the enjoyment is gone. I am exhausted when I wake up in the morning. I am just going through the motions at work. It is almost as if I no longer exist. The sense that I am making a difference and accomplishing something is gone. My anxiety is spinning out of control over everything. I have had several confrontations with my younger partners. That is why I am here. I am lost.*

CHE: *I can see that. It is often the individuals who are the best at what they do and have had the greatest career impact that struggle with the end of things. The first thing we are going to do is see John Halton, the geriatric psychiatrist. We need to get this anxiety and situational depression under control. You and I can then sit down and examine prospects for the future. I assure you the best of our lives are in front of us, not behind.*

I introduced you to RAM to put a human face on the challenges facing individuals closing out their careers. He is fighting several reality checks. The normal aging process has slowed his reaction time and diminished his ability to focus and multitask. He is still able to function at a high level, it just takes longer. Age is also affecting his relationship with technology, robbing him of the benefit of the electronic medical record. This new technology promises to be faster and ensure better outcomes but is often difficult for older physicians to master. The fact that he needs more time to complete the same amount of work leaves less time to think about each patient. The possibility of error is increased, and the anxiety is increased exponentially. This has led to burnout.[1]

The signs in RAM are classic. He is exhausted. The sense of accomplishment is gone. The statement "It's as if I no longer exist" is the most troubling. It signals depersonalization, which always accompanies physician burnout. The referral to a geriatric psychiatrist is Step One.

You ask, *He is 70 years old. Why not see fewer patients and practice at a pace that matches his comfort level?*

Certainly that's a solution, but it would have required insight into the effects of aging. That awareness would have prepared him for the required adjustments. But that option was lost when his reality was "I am still going strong at 70 and have no need to adjust." It wasn't until he was unable to get his work done and began to have confrontations with his colleagues that the anxiety forced him to seek help.

Only the hand that erases can write the truth.

Meister Eckhart

Father Richard Rohr in his book, *Falling Upward: A Spirituality for the Two Halves of Life* (Jossey-Bass, 2013), stresses how drastic these changes need to be. He eloquently makes the point that many of the attributes that make one successful in their career will be a detriment in the second half of life. Careers demand personal sacrifice. Every butcher, baker and candlestick maker is subjugating personal desires and needs to remain competitive and valued. Strong egos and competitive attributes are developed. Success is measured in control, influence and financial reward. Father Rohr teaches us that fundamental changes in perspective and approach must be developed. He calls the process "necessary suffering." He uses the word suffering to emphasize how difficult the process may be. But it is necessary for achieving success in the second half.

RAM's transition from late career to retirement could have benefited from Father Rohr's advice. RAM also has a demographic problem that has made this passage to post-career harder. He is a Boomer. Baby Boomer is the nickname for the generation born in the years following World War II. Some 76 million Americans were born between 1946 and 1964. Countless books and articles have been written on the Boom Generation, trying to identify influences that explain the attitudes and behavior of this population.

The problem is simple. There are too many of us. The system buckled under the strain. Temporary classrooms were needed to accommodate the increased numbers. Each sports tryout or school play had too few spots for the children wanting to participate. The number of applicants for everything—sports, clubs, summer jobs and college—was exploding. Anxiety increased for both parent and child.

From this environment, survival and success demanded that we be competitive with one another. In every endeavor, the question was always, "How do I stack up?" It is so ingrained in our DNA that we are not aware of its presence. As a result, no generation has ever been better prepared for careers than Boomers. The pressure increased when we were told "You are special. You have gifts that ensure a destiny to live lives that your grandparents could not imagine." It all came true. The levels of education and income were the highest in history. This competitive streak, the ability to assess a situation and determine what I need to do to be successful in it, resulted in performance unrivaled in history. We have measured up.

But time moves on. Every day, 10,000 Baby Boomers end a career and begin retirement. The attributes we developed and sacrifices we made to ensure that "we could measure up" are no longer needed. The comparing and competing have served us well. But going forward, they are markers for dissatisfaction and sadness.

The real voyage of discovery consists not in seeking new landscapes but in having new eyes.

Marcel Proust

Proust is right. We need new perspectives to adapt to the changing realities of aging. He is wrong in thinking the insight will come from new eyes. It will come from using different parts of our brains.

The importance of the different regions of the brain in controlling our thoughts and actions has already been introduced. What is also at play is the side of the brain involved. The left and right brain control different aspects of our personality and talents. The science for these observations began in the early 1960s with experiments performed by the neuropsychologist Roger Sperry.[2] Sperry studied a group of patients who had severe epilepsy and were crippled by seizures. Each patient had undergone a surgical procedure that divided the midline connection of the brain to limit the spread of the seizures. In this setting, the two sides of the brain were independent of one another. That allowed Sperry to isolate certain functions to one side or the other. For this elegant work, Sperry won the Nobel Prize in Physiology and Medicine in 1981.

The left brain was found to be involved with language and verbal skills. It was the site of sequencing and linear thinking. Math and logic also reside on the left. The right brain is nonverbal. It involves holistic thinking, big-picture visualization. Feelings, imagination and artistic talent reside on the right.

In the 1990s, pop psychologists misinterpreted the data and declared that each one of us is either a right- or left-brain person. Left brain-dominant individuals are math whizzes. Right brain-dominant individuals are artists and dreamers. But it is not that simple. The two sides of the brain work in synergy.

Many individuals are good at both math and art. There are many unfortunate ones who are bad at both. The exaggeration doesn't work but the science does. For our purposes of navigating transitions, the two sides of the brain offer a template for what we need to jettison and what we need to develop.

It is a matter of time and demands. Both sides of the brain have a voice. At certain times, the voice from one side becomes dominant and drowns out the opposing voice. The left brain is concerned with the external world and its demands on us. The voice is asking, "Can I measure up? What do I have to do to live up to these demands?" This is where we plan and execute. The right brain is concerned with how one feels. "Is this right for me? What is it I truly want to do?" This is where we dream.

The pressures of life force us to be attuned to the voice on the left side of our brains. The demands of everyday life shout at us. The authentic voice on the right is barely audible.

Let's go back to your story. You are walking off the stage at graduation holding the diploma in your hand. A distinguished speaker just told you that you are special and the world needs your talent and perspective. The voice from the right side of your brain is loud and confident. "I have dreams and I can make them come true." You arrive at college. Teachers and counselors are focused on you and your dreams. Everyone is listening. You tell them, "I want to study English, become a writer." They map it out. Here is how you get there. The voice is strong. The vision for the future is clear.

The demands of college life bring a reality check. Academic pressures arise, but the dream lives. Then you arrive home at

Thanksgiving. At dinner on the first night, your father asks, "How are you doing? Do you like school?" You share that you love your courses, especially English and writing. The next line has been been repeated for countless generations. "You know, you can't make a living with an English degree," your father says. "I know we said you can do anything in life but you need to be practical. You can still love writing and poetry and all that stuff but major in something that at least gets you a job and a decent salary. Poets always starve."

The voice in your head starts to fade. Your confidence weakens. This is the start of life's assault on the authentic you.

What follows is reality—love, maybe children, triumph, loss. They are the distractions and the demands of life. There should be no regrets. But the voice, that authentic connection to you, is no longer audible. It is gone.

My mission is to urge you to listen to that voice as you age. The distractions and frenzy of life are waning. A new reality is just ahead. The voice that is linked to dreams and talent can be heard again, if you listen for it. Doubters will say, "It's too late. This type of thinking and hoping, it never works." My response? Tell that to J.K. Rowling. Harry Potter started as that faint voice in her brain.

Our goal from the outset has been to achieve joy and purpose in these later years. Life's pressing demands are gone. You are on your own. Let me repeat myself for emphasis. You are on your own. This is both the beauty and the terror of it all. The pressure is on us to make the years ahead count.

So here we stand at the end of a career, looking into the future through a set of binoculars. The view is out of focus. No amount of adjusting helps. Maybe a new set of more expensive binoculars will clear things up.

Sorry, no. What is needed now are your powers of insight, creativity and imagination. There's your answer. What exactly that looks like is up to you. If you're interested in making the short journey from your left to right brain, read on.

Endnotes

1) A recent article in Forbes magazine written by Robert Pearl, M.D. is excellent on physician burnout and its causes. https://www.forbes.com/sites/robertpearl/2019/07/08/physician-burnout-1/#751a423b119e

2) The article published by Dina Lienhard in 2017 is the best review of Sperry's work. It can be found at: https://embryo.asu.edu/pages/roger-sperrys-split-brain-experiments-1959-1968

Seek out that particular mental attitude
which makes you feel most deeply and vitally
alive, along with which comes the inner voice
which says, "This is the real me," and when
you have found that attitude, follow it.

— William James
The Principles of Psychology

8

On Your Own

Careers provide structure. They have been the source of our values and identity for decades. Leaving them behind will not be easy. There will be anxiety and uncertainty. But done right, this transition to retirement will force us to develop new and more personal values and reward systems. We're on our own.

You say, *OK, I get that when my career is over, things will change whether I like it or not. But I am not comfortable with my changing. I like the person I am. I am not interested in becoming someone else.*

No one is asking you to become someone else. The adjustments we are talking about are changes in perspective, changes in expectations.

Where does this new perspective come from? How do I get it?

It doesn't come from anywhere. It is already inside you. It just needs to be recognized and tapped. We must reconnect with all the positive aspects of ourselves and use them to construct a life. A life that is interesting and rewarding enough to match our careers.

In the spring of '27, something bright and alien flashed across the sky. A young Minnesotan (Charles Lindbergh) who seemed to have nothing to do with his generation, did a heroic thing, and for a moment people set down their glasses in country clubs and speakeasies and thought their old best dreams.

F. Scott Fitzgerald, **Tales of the Jazz Age**

This is where we will start, with our old best dreams. Close your eyes and bring into focus that youth sitting in the back seat of the family car on the way to his first year in college. Both child and parent know this is a rite of passage. Life will never be the same. What did that innocence look and feel like? What talents was the child counting on to measure up? What was his expectation of what life had in store?

Now before you get realistic and tell me that this young man had no idea what the world had in store for him, marvel at the moment. What was special about this youth? I am going to let you have your say. But I want to emphasize that this naïve young person is crucial to the story and the final outcome.

OK, your turn.

What difference does it make what that young version of me thought or dreamed? It was all a mirage, or worse, a cruel, short prelude to a life that never lived up to any shining goal or achievement. At least not enough to say that "dreams came true." Why bring up these memories? They just hurt.

I bring up these memories because this story is not finished. If we are going to use the power of narrative to gain insight and foster change, we need to know where it starts. This young person, with his talents and vision, has the potential to play a vital role as we look to our future.

The decisive moment in successful aging comes with the awareness that you alone are responsible for what this will look like. It should originate from within with no influence from societal norms. This is my story. With this late freedom, I am going to write the last chapters, not with "What is expected of me?" but "What do I expect of myself?" It is the freedom to say, "I don't have to do anything earth-shattering."

That young man riding to college may have been a marvelous clarinet player who loved jazz. This was all forgotten in his career as a banker. But that career is over. The reconnect may be to pick up the clarinet and join a jazz group or simply rekindle a love of music. Even better, play music with a granddaughter. The young man may have loved acting and was successful in school plays. The local theater group is desperate for actors and would welcome newcomers. It could be as simple as season tickets to the theater. The young man may have been a terrific baseball player. His son is now coaching his grandchild's team and needs an assistant. Again, nothing earth-shattering. But reconnecting with that youth allows us to dust off our "old best dreams."

Late-in-life pursuits don't have to be linked to youthful talent. They may arise from out of nowhere or from a desire that has always been there but never acted on. You often hear, "I have always wanted to paint but have been afraid I had no talent and would be embarrassed." Or "I never had the chance to go to college. In high school, history was my favorite subject. I want to take classes but am afraid I won't be able to keep up with people who have been to college."

It seems simple. But if there is one thing life has taught us, it's that it is never simple. Two factors threaten to undermine the best intentions.

The first is **fear of failure**. This is the left brain whispering, "Can you really paint?" For Boomers, it may sound like this: "If you take a class, there will be others in the class with real talent. You know how this ends, with disappointment." In years past, that voice would have been loud enough to scratch the whole deal. But this time is different. We are moving away from this left-brain dominance and its competitive nature. The right brain responds in a firm voice. "I have wanted to do this for years and will regret missing this opportunity. It feels right this time. I may not be good at it but I can accept that if the pursuit brings me pleasure."

Common Mistake of Aging #8

Not accepting the fact that I may no longer be good at something but continue to pursue it for sheer pleasure.

The second factor is **loss of will**. Will is the active link between thought and action. It is the force that allows us to complete actions and desires. It resides primarily in the prefrontal cortex, which we covered in Chapter Three, and is most sensitive to aging. Time weakens will. An individual may have clear thoughts of what they need to accomplish and why, but no action follows. It is more pronounced than just being distracted, although that also occurs. At the extreme, in my dementia patients, it is the loss of the visual image of the sequential steps required to complete even simple problems.

In contrast, Super Agers have preserved will. It is a distinguishing characteristic of this set. If the thought takes hold to accomplish something, they will persist until that something is done. Super Ager SBA, who I introduced in Chapter Four, is going on a trip to France. She is taking French lessons in anticipation of the trip. She is not concerned that she will not be proficient in speaking French. She did it because she thought it would be fun and enhance the entire experience.

The lady who is finally going to pursue her passion for art is not aware of the positive effects that may result. The entire process—the desire, the call, the attendance and the learning—triggers new neural pathways. The brain is energized when asked to connect thought with action. Being aware of the importance of will and the benefit of the desired action may be a link to a healthy aging brain.

Fear of failure and loss of will are two factors that undermine our desire to be productive in our later years. They pale in the face of a third, which if present will keep us from attaining any joy or purpose. It is arrogance. Careers demand that we develop talent and strong egos to match. It requires a confident, competent individual to advise clients in the law, lead any size business or perform a surgical procedure on a sick patient. We are naturally drawn to those individuals. We want them involved in our lives.

The tragic nuance is that one iota of too much ego tips over into arrogance. This is the state in which one is convinced of their superiority over others. I saw this repeatedly in my career as a surgeon. Men and women of superior talent and expertise crossed that fine line and what followed was often disastrous. Relationships with colleagues and friends suffered. Marriages unraveled. Lives of promise spun out of control. One can often pull off this self-centeredness during careers but almost never in retirement. Happiness later in life hinges on diminishing egos and developing valued relationships with others. Arrogance always ends up angry and alone.

We have spent enough time on what works against us once we stop working. It is time to explore what does work and how can we get in on it.

What is graceful aging? Grace is defined as elegance, suppleness or fluidity. When I apply those definitions to aging, the one that fits is suppleness. This connotes a softness and adaptability, traits essential for graceful aging.

Three elements of aging stem from this lightness.

It means softly accepting the phase you are in with no regrets over what is lost, but rather an appreciation for what is left. The softness is actually a misnomer in that is easier to be bitter over lost attributes then tackling the hard work of making a life out of what remains. It means allowing friends and family members to come closer. It means accepting help with the progressive challenges of aging. An example: Asking a daughter to help with the checkbook "to make sure I am not making any mistakes." This willingness to be helped brings loved ones into your life and gives them concrete ways to love you. "I am perfectly capable of doing things myself" is a lonely walk.

Common Mistake of Aging #9

Delaying or refusing to have loved ones involved in the crucial aspects of our lives.

It means constantly being aware of the everyday details in the lives of those you love. Self-absorption often accompanies aging. Being interested and involved with others can offset the isolation that is destructive to the connectedness we crave.

Profiles In Successful Aging

For more than 40 years, RA was a corporate lawyer. Not just a corporate lawyer, but a celebrated one. An academic record of prestigious scholarships, dean's lists and awards was followed by an exemplary career. Life became a series of demands. "We are sending the corporate jet." "We want your opinion here in New York tomorrow morning." "Can you be in London for a meeting next week?" The pressure, pace and challenges led to profound career satisfaction. In those magazines where they rate professionals by reputation and talent, he was always at the top. Surely slowing down would be hard, and retirement could be disastrous.

At age 67, he informed his partners that he would be gone in one year. He would not need an office or secretary. On that day, he bid everyone a heartfelt good-bye and walked out.

If you want to talk to this internationally acclaimed lawyer today, you only have to call his daughter's bakery. This is where he answers the phone and helps her bake cakes. What he really loves is being there when the grandchildren arrive home from school. He says, "I need them and they need me."

He still retains one title, Chief Warden at his church. He readily admits "to being over my head in responsibility."

What RA is saying is, "I no longer need or want the trappings of my law career. I know how to do that. What I am eager to see is how this next chapter of my story plays out." Smaller ego, fewer needs and focusing on others are the elements of his post-career happiness.

APB is 99 years old and living in assisted living in a retirement center. She was happily married for more than 50 years but lost her husband 18 years ago. She has endured multiple transitions in her life. The most compelling was adopting four children after the death of her husband's brother and his wife. She raised them along with her own three children. She was totally devoted to raising these seven children and preparing them for life. After that was accomplished, she turned to traveling and spending every day with her husband. Following his death in 2002, her focus became her children and grandchildren. She has, by necessity, developed an instinct for what is expected of her at this time. Never dwelling on what is lost but "how can I make the best of what I have left?"

Common Mistake of Aging #10

Losing curiosity and, more importantly, losing the fascination with the everyday details of life.

She knows every birthday, coming event, triumph and tragedy for all 36 members of her family. She places herself in their lives daily. If her daughter is having a dinner party, she wants to know who, what, where and how many. She will ask, "Do you have enough salad plates for that many?" This may seem trivial. But what she is really saying is "I love you and am thinking about you." She gave up tennis in her late 80s ("couldn't see the ball anymore") and driving at 92. She loved going to lunches and dinner with family and friends until 96. She now will leave her cottage on occasion but mostly is content to be at home. She is an avid reader and remains curious about everything and everyone. Each child, grandchild and great-grandchild receives Christmas gifts (multiple) from her that are thoughtful and appropriate for age and circumstance. She watches a church service every Sunday and goes shopping Monday afternoon. She is calm, joyful and attentive.

RPR is a 92-year-old retired physician. He was an OB/GYN surgeon in Charlotte for more than 60 years. He is held in such high esteem that his partners insisted on naming the clinic after him. He loved all aspects of his practice and delivered babies into his 60s. Only in his late 70s did he slow down from a busy surgical practice. He continued to assist in surgery until his early 80s. His opinion was sought even in his late 80s. Being a physician was all he asked of life. He was never concerned with investments, the business of medicine or any competing pursuits. He was a doctor and that was enough. His career was marked by a fanatical desire to stay current in medical knowledge and his commitment to the underserved.

Obviously such a long career is unusual, but it worked. When the end finally came, it was accepted with grace and gratitude for the amazing run.

Just after giving up all aspects of practicing medicine, he called and asked if I could come over and answer a few technology questions. I laughed and said, "You are losing it if you think I am a reliable resource on technology." When I arrived, he explained that he wanted my help in signing up for The New England Journal of Medicine's continuing education program. He wanted to keep his license active and needed the credits. I gently reminded him that he was nearly 90 years old and probably had little need to stay current as a physician. He smiled and said, "Chuck, you never know what is going to happen. They might need me to come back. I need to be ready."

RPR's story is important because it points out that strategically slowing down can prolong a career and preserve late vitality. You must understand that a smaller role must be embraced without compromise. This is not a "holding-on" strategy, but a way to keep talents and wisdom alive for the benefit of colleagues and patients.

As different as these three stories are, there are several common themes. The first is that their smaller egos reflected an awareness of others and their needs. The second is that they each allowed loved ones to be integral to their lives. Third, their graceful transition to new realities will ensure relevance in later years. Time forces us to make changes in order to be in stride with our energies and resources. By understanding that, these individuals avoided the anxiety and bitterness that often accompany advancing age and loss. The payoff from these wise decisions and suppleness is calmness and a sense of purpose in new roles going forward.

The search is what anyone would undertake if he were not sunk in the everydayness of his own life. To become aware of the possibility of the search is to be on to something. Not to be onto something is to be in despair.

Walker Percy, *The Moviegoer*

What is this search that Percy is talking about? How do we get on to something and avoid the despair that he warns of?

The transition to late career and retirement offers the ideal time to step back, swallow hard and assess what has been written of your story so far. What has worked and what hasn't? This is also the time to think about the future and the final chapters of this narrative. Will they reflect a person aware of the stage they are in and willing to adjust to new realities? Or will the person play this out in the everydayness of wasted time?

The first step is to PLAN. Short of an untimely death, each of us will have to make that transition from career to retirement. It is inevitable. But as I mentioned in the Prologue, it is astounding: We spend decades planning for a career that may last 25 to 30 years, but give little thought to post-career, which has the potential to last as long or longer. Many of us will plan for the financial demands and where we will live but give little consideration to what we will be doing. What will keep us sharp, and ensure that life will be interesting and valued?

The planning may be as simple as living where you are, immersing yourself in family and traveling with friends. It may involve moving to a college town, where courses allow for intellectual pursuits. It may be more dramatic—a move out West to live on a ranch where the cowgirl and cowboy finally get their chance. You get the picture. It will require planning long before they hand you the gold watch and show you the door.

The second charge is to pay attention. In Chapter Four, we covered the characteristics of Super Agers. A defining characteristic is awareness of others, their situations, their intent. PAYING ATTENTION for us means following that example. It means being involved in the details of the lives of those we love. We learned from 99-year-old APB how sustaining this can be as we lose mobility and options with advanced age.

Your time is limited, so don't waste it living someone else's life.

Steve Jobs

The third and most important element in our search is finding the AUTHENTICITY that Jobs is talking about. We have even created the scientific metaphor of moving from the left brain to the right to create an image of reconnecting with your genuine self. Listen to the voice coming from the right brain and have confidence that the world not only wants but needs to benefit from that unique individual.

At the outset, we established goals worthy of the search on which we embark. We said we want to be valued and cherished until the end. We want to be vitally connected to family and friends. Lastly, we want to experience calm and peace—a sign that we are comfortable with who we are and the lives we have led. This is your story. Make it good.

Teach us to care, not to care and to sit still.

— T. S. Eliot, "Ash Wednesday"

9

Extra Credit

I knew it. You Boomers could not resist the possibility of getting extra credit. Our mission to leave the competitive edge behind and move to our authentic selves may not be taking hold just yet. I will keep trying.

I'll start by introducing the concept of wonder. I am going to borrow the definition of wonder from H. Martyn Evans of Trevelyn College, Durham University, in the United Kingdom.

He defines wonder as "intense and transfiguring attentiveness" that can turn the ordinary into extraordinary. This is a powerful concept when applied to aging.

Life is made up of ordinary individuals doing ordinary things. When we see it as wonder, we see these toils in a different light. The sum of our efforts and struggles are extraordinary. This is true when applied to the late stages of life, when (hopefully) wisdom combines with the preciousness of time to make every day a gift.

Wonder is usually associated with major happenings— moonshots, heart transplants and heroic deeds. They deserve all the historical significance attributed to them. But I contend that these big moments also have a negative side. They make us associate wonder with superhuman feats that only a few are capable of performing. The rest of us are left with the humdrum of commonplace existence.

My new practice has made me a party to human suffering every day. My patients and families struggling with Alzheimer's and related dementias have had their lives pushed to the edge of reason and tolerance. There is no pause or respite, only more decline, more humiliation. And yet in this setting, I see the human spirit at its best—indomitable, defiant and resolute. I see wonder in these travails.

Let me show you what I mean.

PR is 58 years old with early onset Alzheimer's disease. Her problems with memory and cognition began more than eight years ago when she could no longer remember details of her husband's business trips. "Where are you going? How long are you going to be gone?" she'd repeatedly ask him. At first, her husband, TR, thought she wasn't listening. Relating it to menopause became an excuse. It wasn't until her friends confronted him that he began to take the symptoms seriously. TR then noted she was having difficulty communicating. It was as if she knew what she wanted to say but couldn't find the words. When eating, there were times she could not see her plate or utensils. She'd overreach for items. She lost confidence in driving and stopped voluntarily.

Her husband brought her to Memory & Movement Charlotte for an evaluation. After taking a history, performing neuropsychological testing and a physical exam, I had to inform the husband that this was early-onset Alzheimer's disease. He was in shock. He left asking if he could return in a few days, after he "got his thoughts together." Three days later, he returned. "The last three days have been hell," he said. "I have had my pity party and now I am mad. I want you to teach me about this disease and how I can fight it. Doc, I have to warn you. I don't have any give-up in me."

Early-onset Alzheimer's is a different disease, I explained. It affects different parts of the brain than late onset. It affects what she sees and her orientation in space along with memory and cognition. That is why she stops eating abruptly. She loses sight of the plate. She can no longer measure distances, resulting in her overreaching for objects.

He interrupts. "What can I do? Is there anything in my control to slow this down or just make it a little better?"

"Yes," I tell him. "Exercise, social interaction and emotional support can make a difference. If she is depressed or agitated, we can treat that with medication. But the harsh reality is that the disease is progressive and she will get worse."

He asks, "Where are we now? What stage are we in?"

"We are in late stage four," I respond. "There are seven stages."

He asks if there are any predictions as far as how fast it will progress.

The answer is no.

This is where it began. He refused to let the disease take its course without a fight. He called every important person in his life and formed an army. He called it his Army of Angels. "I will need your help to support both of us," he told them. "Help me fight this disease."

Every morning, they were up at 6 and in the gym. She was on the treadmill, then he would train her with yoga and weights. He scheduled trips with friends and family all over the world. He took the neuropsychiatric test home and gave her the same test every day. At first, she improved. I'd get a text message with nothing but a number. It would read 22 that day. Her initial test was 18 out of 30.

This intensity allowed her to remain stable for nearly two years. When the inevitable decline began, it was unbearable for him. She could no longer walk on the treadmill. She could not be left alone. Confusion and fear became constant companions, preventing any travel. Her test scores began to drop. When the disease resisted his efforts, TR began to break down. He'd have unexplained panic attacks, one during a high-level meeting with his bosses in New York. Counseling and medication eliminated the panic attacks but not the heartache. His wife was now often incontinent and asking in his presence, "Where is my husband?"

TR is a planner. He had already researched facilities that would be appropriate for her. He knew he could no longer care for her at home. His mother could no longer handle her when he was away on business. He knew that in the right setting she would have stimulation and better care than hired caregivers could give in the home.

The first weeks apart were excruciating for him even though she adjusted beautifully to the new situation. He gave himself no credit for the super-human efforts he had put forth for four years. He felt only guilt. This feeling slowly ebbed as he became convinced that she was better off now than at home.

We are now five years into the decline. It has had ups and downs, tears and laughter, often at the same time. A bond has been forged between TR and me, the product of trust and the realization that we both love her. His panic and despondency are gone, jettisoned by the dual awareness that she can no longer speak for herself and that it has fallen on us to ensure she is calm, safe, clean and loved.

What does this have to do with wonder?

The transfiguring attentiveness shows itself differently in each of us. In TR, it is in his total submission to her agenda and needs. It has endured through anger, defiance, obsession and defeat, all of which took him to the limits of his own sanity. His battle against the disease has been elevated to the extraordinary by his rage against the decline, and by his dedication to her.

For me, the wonder in this, the transfiguring attentiveness, is being so deeply immersed in the struggle. Without the wonder and resilience of the human spirit, it is all tragedy and despair. After the ordeal is over, the caregivers have been transformed. They are emboldened by having survived and know that life has nothing more tragic to throw at them. The experience, the suffering, has opened avenues of emotion and understanding that has made them more aware, calmer, stronger.

This added dimension of the human experience is the gift that wonder offers to those who pay attention.

You may think that TR and his story are rare. It is not. His approach was unique but the courage and resilience he exhibited is not. My caregivers and patients (yes, the patients) show these qualities every day. Their late years have been hijacked by Alzheimer's disease. But their spirit should be an example to us of what extraordinary really means.

I know, I already had one final thought. I promise this to be my final, final thought. The quote at the beginning of this chapter by T.S. Eliot from his poem "Ash Wednesday" has always spoken to me. It probably stems from my never being able to "sit still." To me, that quality has never had more meaning than late in one's life. It forces us to connect with our past and present, but it is really about the future. It offers a solitary, personal look at the time ahead and what will be needed, what will be valued.

"Teach us to care." This speaks directly to one's story. Caring about this one life I have. Valuing the thoughts I have and acting on them. Thinking and caring for those we love.

"Teach us not to care." This speaks to living up to outside expectations and demands. We have already done this. Post-career offers a chance to explore and connect with different aspects of ourselves. Carrying baggage from previous phases of our lives will prevent the discovery of our authentic self that promises to make this last stage new and interesting.

"And to sit still." This is the hard one. It drills into our desire to be free from anxiety and turmoil. "Sitting still" is the metaphor for achieving the peace we long for desperately.

An Essay on Anxiety

Before you go, there is an unfinished piece of business. Your asking me to "sit still" has reminded me. You have talked continually through the book about anxiety and how destructive it is in our lives. You told us where it comes from. I want to know how to get rid of it.

I can't promise getting rid of it. Let's shoot for managing it for a start. Understanding it better, absolutely.

Anxiety was born in the same moment as mankind. And since we will never master it, we will have to learn to live with it – just as we live with storms.
—Brazilian writer Paulo Coelho—

My interest in anxiety stems from my patients with dementia. As they decline, their social boundaries and insight fade. They are unable to control their thoughts and subsequent actions. Obsessions, misunderstandings and raw emotions are allowed to roam unchecked in their brains, all of it a laboratory for anxiety.

A major challenge for any physician caring for patients with Alzheimer's and related dementia is controlling agitation and aggressive behavior. If not controlled, the patients can be a danger to those caring for them and themselves. Anxiety is a major source of the anger. If we can calm the anxiety, there is a better chance to control the unwanted behavior.

At Memory & Movement Charlotte, we see patients with Alzheimer's, Parkinson's and other psychiatric illnesses. Some have memory loss, some not. We began to see a common thread. Anxiety is a major factor in the behavior of all our patients whether they have memory issues or not.

Then the epiphany came. I realized that all of us harbor anxiety at some level. It affects our thoughts, fears and actions every day without our knowing how, why or where it comes from. We learned the common sources of the anxiety in Chapter Four. Each stressful origin has its unique entrance into our lives, requires a different approach and will exit in its own way. Let me explain.

First, let's define anxiety again. It is a painful uneasiness. The key word is painful. Humans do not tolerate pain and will do most anything to avoid or eliminate it. This is why these feelings of unrest have such influence on our thoughts and actions. It is also the reason they must be addressed.

The first source of anxiety entered our being on the day we were born. It is in our DNA. For most of time, it has been a marker for survival. Being anxious made one more aware of danger and less apt to take risk. Nervous individuals were more likely to survive and multiply. This sequence has played out for countless generations, with each successive generation being more anxious. At some point, it stopped being a marker for longevity and became the opposite, a trait associated with shorter lives.

Anxiety is not necessarily a negative. Some of the edgiest individuals I have known have been the brightest and most productive. That uneasiness with the present can be a catalyst for creativity and innovation. Nervous individuals never sit still.

OK, I got it. I was born with it. Now what do I do about it?

At Memory & Movement Charlotte, we care for numerous patients with personality disorders. The most common is Generalized Anxiety Disorder. These are individuals born with excessive anxiety that affects them dramatically every day. It is rare that these patients are aware of the source of their anxiety or how it affects them. They have no clue how to manage it. Because of this profile, they offer us insight into anxiety in its extreme. If there are strategies that work in this setting, they have the potential to help all of us.

In our counseling sessions with these patients, we make three points. First, we reveal the source of the excessive distress. You were born with this. It is with you now and will be with you forever. You are not weak. This is a trait you inherited, like blue eyes or a beautiful singing voice. It is you.

Second, the tendency that you have had throughout life to assign your anxiety to perceived challenges is wrong. It was never the tryout, the test or the wedding that triggered the uneasiness. Although they may enhance the distress, the lion's share was always inside.

Lastly, we want the patient to reexamine their lifelong relationship with anxiousness. The realization that it has always been with me and always will be should be a release. A release from the burden of feeling this is a weakness, a flaw. A release from the misconception that if I can just get through the upcoming pressures that everything will be "back to normal." Being anxious is normal for this group of patients.

Individuals with Generalized Anxiety Disorder will often need counseling and sometimes medication to manage their exaggerated uneasiness. Their gift is reminding us that painful uneasiness is a part of life. Awareness of its origin and the fact we all share it is a good start toward managing it.

The second way anxiety enters our lives is through traumatic life experiences. Mike Tyson has warned us about these setbacks in an earlier chapter. Each of our lives has had ups and downs, triumphs and failures. These events may be life-altering or simply an accumulation of things that did not work out. The life-altering trauma often requires professional help to work through.

We are going to focus on less tragic occurrences but ones that have left emotional scars. For example, it may be remembrances of a failed love affair, a business calamity or a flawed relationship with a parent. The anxiety associated with these memories will continue to affect our behavior, future decisions and internal calmness until addressed.

The times in our lives when we were unsure, frightened and confronted adversity, the events that left scars, are the times that shaped us profoundly. Their effect is not in the past, it is present. Anxiety prevents us from revisiting these painful episodes. It stops us from understanding what happened and how we were changed by them. We are left with the pain and uneasiness but without a way to expunge it. Anger is often the result. Confronting these memories is difficult. The anxiety is there but time has hidden the source of the distress. This is a coping mechanism that allows us to suppress painful memories and emotions so we can function. It is only when something triggers the memory do we revisit the dissonance.

Anxiety increases with age. It may be the number of times that life has thrown us a curve. It may be that we are more fragile and have lost some of the ability to recover from disappointments and emotional injuries. Whatever the reason, we long for less turmoil and more tranquility. How can this be done?

First, one has to reopen the muted memory and relive the painful episodes. It must come into sharp focus, and the anxiety unleashed has to be anticipated. Your initial response will always be to get away from the angst. "I don't want to think about this now, I will confront this later" is the internal voice that is heard. But if the resolve is strong enough, the hurt will be relived, the anxiety endured and a resolution reached. It is as if the anxiety is burned off by the intensity of seeing it again.

The anxiety that is hardest to move beyond is attached to memories linked to regret. Regrets are stored with excess emotion in the human brain. Every life has regrets. They may be related to failed relationships or flawed decisions that proved costly. Actions that were hurtful to others also qualify. These emotional memories can and often do creep back into our consciousness in later years.

Coming to peace with regrets always involves forgiveness. The wisdom we have earned over a lifetime may allow us to forgive parents or family members for painful memories. Reliving these difficult periods with the intention of achieving a truce may reveal realities that were hidden by anger. These revelations may lead to an understanding that the individuals involved had demons, their own regrets, which were responsible for the flawed behavior. Forgiveness may follow.

In the instances when we are responsible for an injustice or harm, the stakes are higher and the regret deeper. The fact that we once fell below a standard that we now have set for ourselves or that youth prevented our seeing the harmful potential of an action should not plague us forever. We must be able to forgive ourselves. Forgiving ourselves is complicated and involves more than reliving and understanding. It requires redemption. An act to offset the offense is required to release us from the painful memory.

The act, the atonement, should be personal and proportional. It could be as simple as a vow to be more aware of the burdens of others and to act appropriately. It may be that regrets over not being involved in your children's lives at crucial times is replaced by being involved in your grandchildren's lives. You get the idea.

The anxiety created by regret subtly undermines joy and calm in later years. These ideas on anxiety and the process of understanding and addressing it are presented to engender introspection and reevaluation. They are meant to be a gentle push to revisit earlier chapters of our stories that may contain painful recollections. They are meant to be a start, not the answer, to making the final chapters calmer and more joyful.

Lessons From COVID-19

My patients with dementia have been affected dramatically by the response to the Corona virus. The quarantine, shutdowns and distancing have affected all of us. But those who are experiencing memory problems have been impacted out of proportion. The social isolation and disrupted schedules have resulted in a decline in both cognition and memory. The patients lose perspective of time and place. Short-term memory declines and confusion is a daily occurrence. The confusion is often accompanied by anxiety and agitation.

Our goal at Memory & Movement Charlotte is to keep our patients calm, safe, clean and loved. As the dementia progresses, as it always does, keeping the patients calm becomes more difficult. The patients can no longer solve simple problems and are easily distracted. Attention spans are short and following instructions is no longer consistent.

These changes result in the loss of purpose and context. The patients will often ask "What's next? What am I supposed to be doing now?" They become anxious in the wake of this void.

To offset these declines, we turn to techniques that divert the patient from upsetting situations and replace them with simpler pursuits. That is where the five senses come in.

The five senses are sensory organs that respond to stimuli from the environment. They are touch, smell, hearing, sight and taste. They differ from the conscious interactions that arise in the upper layers of the brain called the cortex. They are independent of consciousness and link us to our surroundings, often without our being aware of their role. We have already introduced the prefrontal cortex and its role in awareness and allowing us to solve problems. The irony is that the evolution of the prefrontal cortex and our ability to remember, fear and plan comes with a price. That price is anxiety. In a complicated connection, the five senses are the antidote to the enhanced anxiety housed in the cortex of the frontal lobe.

Alzheimer's and related dementias attack the frontal lobe and the cortex throughout the brain, extinguishing the societal boundaries housed there. Anxiety and agitation are no longer rationally controlled. The five senses are used to offset the loss of cortical influence.

Touch can be used effectively to calm. Holding the patient's hands firmly or placing one's forehead to the patient's forehead is uniquely calming. Making the patient aware of the sun's effect on their skin or the feeling of shade is diverting and calming.

Music is a major source of diversion. There is a specific area of the brain that houses music, and it is surprisingly preserved until late in the disease. Music from the patient's youth is the most effective. My patients in their 80s and 90s respond to big band sounds immediately. Patients will listen quietly while being read to even though later they cannot remember what has been read. In that moment, the words have meaning. This may take the form of asking the patient a question and taking the time for them to communicate their feelings.

The sense of smell and taste are effective in calming but often require cueing. This involves consciously making the patient aware of smells, flowers, cooking, or making a point to slow down while eating and taste the food being eaten. A patient who is anxious will often respond to snacks and specifically sweets. One small bite of a Snickers may rescue a whole afternoon.

Being aware of the external stimuli that trigger the five senses will be rewarded by moments of calm and joyful interaction.

Okay, I got it. But what does this have to do with the Coronavirus?

The quarantine and social isolation forced on us by COVID-19 compelled us to be creative in keeping our patients calm and free of agitation. It also made us aware of the composing effect it had on caregivers. We then made the leap that all of us could benefit from the quiet and escape from the noise and uneasiness in our daily lives. By being aware of the deep positive effect that the five senses can offer us, we can stake out stress-free havens that allow us to recharge and re-arm.

Eastern medicine stresses the benefits of meditation. That's another name for consciously ignoring the anxiety-producing signals from the frontal lobe and deriving a calmness from the blankness created. We can achieve the same benefit through cleverly using the five senses with the added bonus of being able to share the process with others.

The stress-free havens may simply be taking walks, making use of our eyes and ears and consciously avoid thinking. They may be sessions when we read to our spouses. They may involve more touching, hugging or hand-holding, which we humans continue to need throughout our lives. The first sensation that we experienced was the sense of touch. The benefits – the calming and feeling of connectedness – never wane.

Slowing down and actively being aware of our surroundings is crucial to successful aging. The left side of the brain always wants to control and set the agenda. It will rob one of appreciating the sights and sounds of the day. It will tell you that you don't have time to do what you want to do but remind you that "things need to get done." Listen to that soft voice rising from the right side of the brain. It is whispering, "There is magic all around us—watch, listen, hear, smell and taste it."

Epilogue

By this time, I should have nothing left to say on aging. I don't. It's all in the book. Time, science, transitions, anxiety and wonder are all in there. I started out to write a book on aging for the general public. My goal was to share the perspective I gained from a surgical career that took a sharp turn late into geriatrics and dementia. I especially wanted to support my observations and recommendations with science that was easily understood and precisely applied. You will be the judge of whether I have succeeded. My final hope is that each of us will realize that we are writing a story, our story. If we value it and are willing to adjust to the realities brought on by aging, then the final chapters will reflect that we hit our stride. We made time count.

Two loose ends need to be tied.

The first is the fate of the tremor. The shaking that shortened my surgical career and opened up this late-life passion. It now is in both hands. On occasion, I will have to set something down quickly to avoid a calamity. Even so, I am happy to report that it has not progressed to a disability. The tremor and I have an understanding. If it allows me to do anything I want, I won't freak out over the occasional mishap.

The second loose end is the fate of the Memory Center. As I shared, we started with my wife, Mary, and me in 800 square feet of office space. We had no patients and no idea what success would look like. We were aware that a nonprofit in a medical setting had an uncertain future.

The demand for expertise in dementia has been the driving force behind our dramatic growth. We now have more than 1,200 patients as well as 3,000 caregivers under our care. Each month, the number of new patients and families seeking help is increasing.

To care for this exploding population, I have been fortunate to recruit a team of professionals that shares the vision and passion for this mission. We now have four teams, each led by a physician. Each team has a slightly different focus. One is led by a neurologist, one a psychiatrist and a third by a movement specialist. The final team is led by a dusted-off heart surgeon, now geriatrician. The teams are supported by medical personnel that includes a physician assistant and six registered nurses. We have seven administrative staff, including an executive director as well as director of community engagement and development.

The care of patients with dementia and their families is difficult and demanding. The days are long, complicated and often emotional. The culture is one of service. Each team member understands the commitment and possesses both the expertise and access to resources that are required to make the lives of our patients and families better. It has been a late-life gift to be part of this.

The number of patients we have seen with Parkinson's disease has steadily climbed from the outset. Half of these patients will have some degree of dementia. In response to this demand, we have added movement to memory as a primary focus. This is reflected in our new name, Memory & Movement Charlotte.

The incidence of Alzheimer's disease and Parkinson's disease has exploded in our aging population. Any success we have experienced is the result of our Time and Attention Model. This has allowed us to concentrate expertise and resources against these two diseases and given us time to listen and understand.

For me personally, it has been the most rewarding phase of my medical career. As I stated in the dedication, the patients with dementia and the families caring for them have shown me the best of what human beings are capable of. I thank them sincerely for allowing me to be a part of their struggle for patience, strength and compassion in the face of despair.

MEMORY & MOVEMENT
CHARLOTTE
Navigating complexities. Together.

Memory & Movement Charlotte
300 Billingsley Road, #108
Charlotte, NC 28211

Phone: (704) 577-3186
Fax: (704) 626-2701
Email: email@mmclt.org
Website: www.mmclt.org

The sale of this book will support Memory & Movement Charlotte, a nonprofit medical practice. The book sells for $25. To learn more about the Center, please visit the website, call or email.

Copies of *Much Abides: A Survival Guide for Aging Lives* are for sale in Charlotte at Park Road Books, Traditions, and Memory & Movement Charlotte. You can also order it online at www.amazon.com and at other booksellers.

To schedule a program, book signing, or media interview with Dr. Edwards, call (704) 575-6308 or email: garfieldken3129@gmail.com.

About the Author

DR. CHUCK EDWARDS and his wife, Mary, founded Memory & Movement Charlotte, a nonprofit medical practice treating Alzheimer's, Parkinson's and other forms of dementia, in 2013.

He continues to see patients and help families navigate the unique demands of these dread diseases. This late-life mission has been the source of his interest in successful aging.

Chuck and Mary Edwards live in Charlotte, N.C., and have three adult children and eight grandchildren.

This is his first book.

CPSIA information can be obtained
at www.ICGtesting.com
Printed in the USA
JSHW030910310822
29981JS00004B/17